STERLING BIOGRAPHIES

ALBERT EINSTEIN

The Miracle Mind

Tabatha Yeatts

STERLING CHILDREN'S BOOKS

New York

For Ben with love —T. Y.

Acknowledgments
With thanks to Barry Peckham, Latanya Walker, Catherine
Wingfield-Yeatts, Ariana Yeatts-Lonske, Dashiell Yeatts-Lonske,
Elena Yeatts-Lonske, and Harry W. Yeatts, Jr.

STERLING CHILDREN'S BOOKS
New York

An Imprint of Sterling Publishing
387 Park Avenue South
New York, NY 10016

STERLING CHILDREN'S BOOKS and the distinctive Sterling Children's Books logo are trademarks of
Sterling Publishing Co., Inc.

© 2007 by Tabitha Yeatts
Designed for Simon Says Design! by Frieda Christofides
Image research by Susan Schader

ISBN 978-1-4027-3228-7 (paperback)
ISBN 978-1-4027-4950-6 (hardcover)

Library of Congress Cataloging-in-Publication Data

Yeatts, Tabatha.
    Albert Einstein : the miracle mind / Tabatha Yeatts.
        p. cm. -- (Sterling biographies)
    Includes bibliographical references and index.
    ISBN 978-1-4027-4950-6
    ISBN 978-1-4027-3228-7 (pbk.)
    1. Einstein, Albert, 1879-1955--Juvenile literature. 2. Physicists--Biography--Juvenile
literature. I. Title.

QC16.E5Y43 2007
530.092--dc22
[B]
                                        2007003517

Distributed in Canada by Sterling Publishing
c/o Canadian Manda Group, 165 Dufferin Street
Toronto, Ontario, Canada M6K 3H6
Distributed in the United Kingdom by GMC Distribution Services
Castle Place, 166 High Street, Lewes, East Sussex, England BN7 1XU
Distributed in Australia by Capricorn Link (Australia) Pty. Ltd.
P.O. Box 704, Windsor, NSW 2756, Australia

For information about custom editions, special sales, and premium and corporate purchases,
please contact Sterling Special Sales at 800-805-5489 or specialsales@sterlingpublishing.com.

Printed in China

Lot #:
10 9 8 7 6 5 4 3
12/11

www.sterlingpublishing.com/kids

Contents

Events in the Life of Albert Einstein

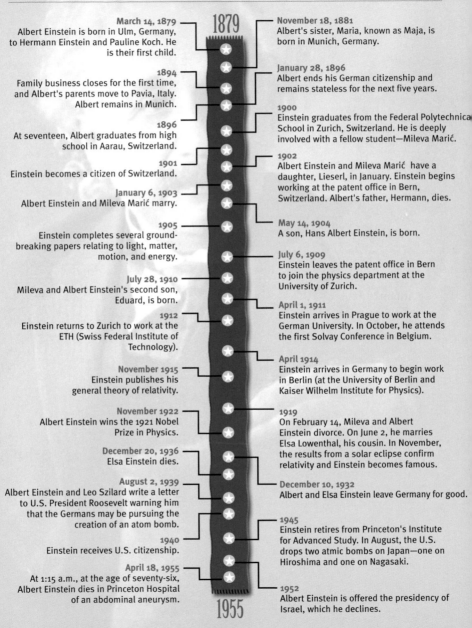

1879

March 14, 1879
Albert Einstein is born in Ulm, Germany, to Hermann Einstein and Pauline Koch. He is their first child.

November 18, 1881
Albert's sister, Maria, known as Maja, is born in Munich, Germany.

1894
Family business closes for the first time, and Albert's parents move to Pavia, Italy. Albert remains in Munich.

January 28, 1896
Albert ends his German citizenship and remains stateless for the next five years.

1900
Einstein graduates from the Federal Polytechnical School in Zurich, Switzerland. He is deeply involved with a fellow student—Mileva Marić.

1896
At seventeen, Albert graduates from high school in Aarau, Switzerland.

1902
Albert Einstein and Mileva Marić have a daughter, Lieserl, in January. Einstein begins working at the patent office in Bern, Switzerland. Albert's father, Hermann, dies.

1901
Einstein becomes a citizen of Switzerland.

January 6, 1903
Albert Einstein and Mileva Marić marry.

1905
Einstein completes several ground-breaking papers relating to light, matter, motion, and energy.

May 14, 1904
A son, Hans Albert Einstein, is born.

July 6, 1909
Einstein leaves the patent office in Bern to join the physics department at the University of Zurich.

July 28, 1910
Mileva and Albert Einstein's second son, Eduard, is born.

April 1, 1911
Einstein arrives in Prague to work at the German University. In October, he attends the first Solvay Conference in Belgium.

1912
Einstein returns to Zurich to work at the ETH (Swiss Federal Institute of Technology).

April 1914
Einstein arrives in Germany to begin work in Berlin (at the University of Berlin and Kaiser Wilhelm Institute for Physics).

November 1915
Einstein publishes his general theory of relativity.

1919
On February 14, Mileva and Albert Einstein divorce. On June 2, he marries Elsa Lowenthal, his cousin. In November, the results from a solar eclipse confirm relativity and Einstein becomes famous.

November 1922
Albert Einstein wins the 1921 Nobel Prize in Physics.

December 20, 1936
Elsa Einstein dies.

December 10, 1932
Albert and Elsa Einstein leave Germany for good.

August 2, 1939
Albert Einstein and Leo Szilard write a letter to U.S. President Roosevelt warning him that the Germans may be pursuing the creation of an atom bomb.

1945
Einstein retires from Princeton's Institute for Advanced Study. In August, the U.S. drops two atmic bombs on Japan—one on Hiroshima and one on Nagasaki.

1940
Einstein receives U.S. citizenship.

April 18, 1955
At 1:15 a.m., at the age of seventy-six, Albert Einstein dies in Princeton Hospital of an abdominal aneurysm.

1952
Albert Einstein is offered the presidency of Israel, which he declines.

1955

A Legendary Physicist

Einstein is great . . . because he has shown us our world in truer perspective and has helped us to understand a little more clearly how we are related to the universe around us.
—*Nobel Laureate Arthur Holly Compton*

Albert Einstein's groundbreaking scientific discoveries made people call him a genius. As a result, many people have wondered about the source of his brilliance. Were his parents really smart? Was his brain especially big, or different? Was Albert Einstein doing arithmetic as an infant?

Albert Einstein himself said not to bother trying to uncover where his special intelligence came from because he claimed he didn't have exceptional smarts. What he did have, he said, was stubbornness, perseverance, and curiosity.

Einstein took his desire to understand the universe and struggled with physics problems until he was able to offer the public a new concept of how the universe worked. Very few people in history have profoundly affected the way people see their world the way Einstein did.

But it isn't just his amazing scientific accomplishments that make Albert Einstein unforgettable. His strong desire to help others, his willingness to stand up for his beliefs, and his memorable comments also keep the Albert Einstein legend alive decades after his death.

CHAPTER 1

Beginnings

Little Albert is so fondly remembered by us; he was so sweet and good, and we have to repeat his amusing ideas again and again.
—Einstein's grandmother Koch

Albert Einstein was an unusual child—a late talker who echoed himself and preferred to play by himself. His gifts were just beginning to take shape. Some observe that Einstein's talents weren't obvious in childhood.

Simple personality traits such as doing things one's own way, thinking "outside the box," and even just wondering about the world might just have been put to use in extraordinary ways in Einstein's case.

Albert's ancestors on both sides were Jewish. His many-greats-grandfather Einstein wasn't an Einstein at all— he was an Ainstein! For some reason, Moises Ainstein's descendants changed the first letter of Ainstein to an "E" to make it Einstein. Otherwise, this book would be titled *Albert Ainstein*.

Albert's father, Hermann Einstein, was a good-natured entrepreneur who struggled to keep a business afloat in order to provide for his family.

Albert's father, Hermann Einstein, was born in 1847, in Buchau, Germany. Hermann was bright and good at mathematics, although his family did not have the funds to send him to a university. He also liked to consider problems from many different angles, something that Albert did with great success. Pauline Koch, Albert's mother, was born in Cannstatt, Germany, in 1858. She had a great love of music, which she passed down to her son. Notably, Pauline was said to have a "sound native wit" and her eyes had a "waggish twinkle" that many people also associated with Albert.

Moving to a Town of Mathematicians

New opportunities available for German Jews, plus the rise of the **industrial revolution**, drew Jews such as the Einsteins from smaller towns to bigger cities. The nearest city to Buchau was Ulm, a very old city whose walls were being torn down to accommodate all the incoming residents. Interestingly enough, Ulm's motto, *Ulmenses sunt mathematici* ("the people of Ulm are mathematicians"), would prove true for its most famous son.

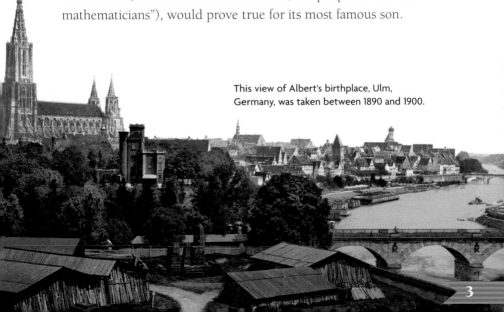

This view of Albert's birthplace, Ulm, Germany, was taken between 1890 and 1900.

3

This photograph shows the home in Ulm where Albert Einstein was born. The Einsteins moved away to Munich when Albert was a toddler.

Pauline and Hermann had their first child, Albert, in Ulm, on March 14, 1879, at 11:30 a.m. The morning after Albert was born, his father went to Ulm's town hall to register his birth. For their religion, Hermann, Pauline, and the new baby were listed as "Israelitic" (Jewish).

When Albert was about a year old, the family moved to Munich to set up an electrical engineering company. Then, on November 18, 1881, the Einsteins had another child, a girl named Maria, whom they all called Maja.

Albert was known for repeating himself until he was at least seven years old. He would think of what he wanted to say, try it out quietly to himself, and then say it out

Maja believed that his early repetition was a reflection of the thoroughness of his thinking.

A Late Talker

Albert was slow to start speaking and did not talk until he was two. This concerned his parents, but once their son started talking, he had interesting things to say. In 1881, Pauline's mother said in a letter after a visit to Munich that "Little Albert is so fondly remembered by us; he was so sweet and good, and we have to repeat his amusing ideas again and again."

Just before Maja was born, the new big brother was told that he would have a little sister to play with, but when he saw her, he asked disappointedly, "Yes, but where does it have its small wheels?" Biographer Albrecht Fölsing says that the **Yiddish** words they used for "little girl" (*madele*) and "small wheels" (*radele*) were similar enough that young Albert could have been making a clever comment on the rhyming sounds—or, more likely, it was a simple misunderstanding. Hearing ahead of time that he would have someone to play with, he may have been expecting a toy. Either way, by now the two-year-old Albert was definitely talking.

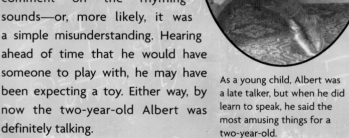

As a young child, Albert was a late talker, but when he did learn to speak, he said the most amusing things for a two-year-old.

loud. The household maid called Albert "stupid" due to this habit, and he might have even thought of himself as slow. Maja believed that his early repetition was a reflection of the thoroughness of his thinking. Although his parents might have been worried about his speech, they still had confidence in his abilities.

Maja later wrote that Albert was taught early to be self-reliant. At age three or four he was allowed to walk along Munich's busiest streets—at first, with someone showing him where to go, but then with someone just watching him from afar, where they could not be seen. Albert carefully looked both ways at intersections and crossed without nervousness.

Even during playtime, Albert was content to play alone. He just wasn't interested in the rowdy outdoor games that most of his cousins and neighbors played. When he was very young, he preferred to sail a small boat in a pail of water or play with chickens and pigeons. Later, he enjoyed doing puzzles and building houses of cards that went up to fourteen card stories

This photograph shows the New City Hall in Munich, c. 1890 to 1900. As a confident child, Albert, at age three or four, walked these streets by himself with an adult watching from afar.

high. Although Albert liked to play alone or with his sister, he occasionally joined group games. He was considered to be the natural choice for umpire or anything that involved settling disagreements because he was regarded as a fair person. His sister, Maja, felt this ability showed that he was able to think objectively at a young age.

Although Albert might have been thought of as an evenhanded person, it didn't mean that he was always even-tempered. He would sometimes have severe temper tantrums, which were said to be inherited from his grandfather Koch. When Albert was five years old, he was taught by a home tutor—until the young student grabbed a chair and tried to strike his teacher, who ran away and never returned. When he was about seven, Albert's temper tantrums ended, which must have been a relief for everyone.

Good friends for life: Albert and his younger sister, Maja, had a close relationship.

Early Interests

At the same time that Albert began his home education, he also began to take violin lessons. Pauline, a skillful pianist, encouraged his musical studies, which continued until he was thirteen. Even after his studies ended, Albert would continue to play violin his whole life. It both relaxed and inspired him—he was sometimes able to solve problems that he mulled over in his head as he played his stringed instrument.

When Albert was about six, he had an important experience that influenced his fascination with the natural world. He was sick in bed when his father, Hermann, brought home a compass to amuse his son. The young boy was struck by the fact that no matter which way the compass was turned, the needle always pointed in the same direction. Prior to seeing the compass, he had assumed that things moved only when other things touched them. But here, an invisible force moved the needle. Albert

realized that there were exciting mysteries to learn from the compass. This insight fueled his inquisitive nature, which would prove so vital in the years to come.

Albert's scientific imagination was kindled by the unseen force behind the movement of a compass needle.

CHAPTER 2

School Days

You sit there in the back row smiling, and that violates the feeling of respect that a teacher needs from his class.

—Albert's Greek professor

On October 1, 1886, seven-year-old Albert began attending his first school. Since there were no Jewish schools, his parents placed him in the *Volksschule*, a Catholic elementary school, with more than two thousand students. Albert was accepted directly into second grade, where he had a teacher who disciplined with *Tatzen* — whacks on the hands— and expected quick answers from his students. Unfortunately, Albert preferred to think about things before responding. Nevertheless, the young student received top grades in his class more than once.

The first school that Albert attended was the *Volksschule*, which was located in Munich. This photo shows a view of the Old Town Hall in Munich between 1890 and 1900.

The Star of David is a six-pointed star that is considered an emblem of Judaism. Jewish children were given religious instructions from the Torah (the first 5 books of Moses), which is shown lying under the Star of David.

As the only Jewish student in his class, Albert felt like an outsider and faced **anti-Semitic** behavior from his classmates, especially after school. At home he might also have felt like an outsider among his cousins. He didn't like to play games that were very physical and he was called "Goody-Goody," perhaps because of his family's rule that he had to finish his homework before he could play. But his relationship with his parents and his sister was strong and would remain a great support for him.

A Classical Education

When Albert was nine years old, he enrolled in Munich's Luitpold Gymnasium, which taught students up through high school. The school's name may sound as if he might have studied physical education all day long, but "gymnasium" is actually the German word for "secondary school." The Luitpold had a heavy focus on the study of languages—Latin and Greek, in particular. Students also studied German, naturally enough, and French. Albert especially enjoyed learning Latin because of the logic of its grammar. Greek was not a favorite of his, perhaps because of his Greek professor, who once informed him in front of the class that

As a young student at Munich's Luitpold Gymnasium, Albert studied several languages, including German, Latin, and Greek.

Albert would not amount to anything. A confrontation with his Greek professor would prove pivotal later on in his life.

Another subject that Albert enjoyed was his religious instruction. Although Albert's family was Jewish, they did not follow Jewish traditions at home. They did not celebrate Jewish holidays or rites. However, all children in the region were required to have religious instruction, so Albert's parents arranged for him to have a Judaism tutor. He studied religion very seriously for the first few years, and stopped eating pork because it is a forbidden food according to Jewish law. He also made up some short hymns, which he would sing to himself.

When Albert was about ten years old, his parents invited a

Polish medical student named Max Talmud to dinner. Talmud and Albert's uncles Caesar Koch and Jakob Einstein would greatly stimulate Albert's private learning. Even though Albert was only ten, Max found that they could already have serious academic discussions. Impressed by young Albert's intelligence and interest, Max brought him many scientific and mathematical books. Albert devoured them all, so Max kept bringing more.

Hermann also brought his son math books, and one summer Albert sat for days on end solving problems and proving **theorems** in those textbooks. He referred to his geometry book as his "holy book."

By the time Albert reached his thirteenth birthday, he became disillusioned with organized religion. During the course of his studies, he could not reconcile his scientific and religious teachings, which disappointed him. So he decided not to participate in the confirmation ceremony for Jewish boys turning thirteen (called a *bar mitzvah*) after all.

Albert, at 13, chose not to have a *bar mitzvah* ceremony. This photograph shows the preparations for a modern *bar mitzvah*, where a young man turning 13 accepts adult religious responsibilities and is officially accepted into the Jewish community.

Einstein's mathematical exploration was significant not only for how much he learned, but for his early questioning of mathematical knowledge. Uncle Jakob pointed out the Pythagorean theorem to his nephew, who, after spending three weeks thinking about it, came up with a

The Pythagorean Theorem

In geometry, the Pythagorean theorem is an equation that allows you to find the length of a hypotenuse (the distance between the two end points of a right triangle). The theory states that in a right triangle, if the length of each leg of the triangle (called a and b) is multiplied by itself (squared) and the two squared lengths are added together, the total will equal the hypotenuse (called c) squared. Mathematically, the equation then reads:

$$a^2 + b^2 = c^2.$$

This is the most fundamental theorem in mathematics, and it was named after the Greek mathematician and philosopher Pythagoras of Samos, who was thought to be the first to prove it.

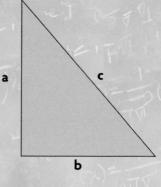

proof for it. Albert's ability to consider the possibility that what was already known might be incorrect or incomplete would lead him down the path to make new discoveries later.

Among the other books that Max brought to Albert was a work by Aaron Bernstein that described how the author imagined it would be to travel through a telegraph line with an electrical signal. Later, when Albert was fifteen, he would wonder what it would be like to ride on a wave of light. His pondering of this question would help lead him to his famous "special theory of relativity."

Young Albert was becoming so well versed in math that Max

couldn't keep up with him, so he started bringing philosophy books instead. As difficult as these philosophers were to read, Albert understood them. A particular favorite of his was Immanuel Kant, a German philosopher who lived from 1724 to 1804. Kant's *Critique of Pure Reason*, first published in 1781, stated that people cannot know things as they are, only as they appear to be.

Even as a young man, Albert enjoyed reading the works of the German philosopher Immanuel Kant, shown in this undated engraving.

Although Albert was making great strides with his studies outside of school, he didn't enjoy his classes at the Luitpold. Aside from its lack of emphasis in his favorite subjects, namely math and physics, it also had a militaristic atmosphere that young Albert disliked. Albert's father's "free-thinking" style may have helped to encourage Albert's blossoming distaste for authority. Nevertheless, Albert managed to continue his studies without too much trouble until his parents decided to leave Germany and move to Italy.

Changes at Home

Hermann and Jakob's electrical engineering company had done well in the early years and had grown to two hundred employees. The company had even supplied the famous Bavarian Oktoberfest with its first electrical lighting in 1885. Albert's uncle Jakob had designed a number of dynamos and electric meters and, together with a number of employees, they held six **patents**.

His ingenuity inspired Albert, who knew enough about what they were doing to explain how a telephone worked to his class and to help out at the company on occasion.

Early on, Albert's father and uncle had some success with their electrical company, supplying lighting for events such as Oktoberfest, which were celebrated in German beer gardens similar to the one depicted in this 1914 photograph.

But it was difficult for a small engineering company to have enough money to compete with giant firms that were starting to monopolize the field. The Einsteins tried hard to keep their business afloat by borrowing money from relatives, but in 1894, the company closed its doors.

It was around this time that an Italian colleague of the Einsteins encouraged them to go to Italy, because it was a better place for a small engineering company. Convinced, the Einsteins made the decision to move to Pavia, Italy. But Hermann and Pauline felt that Albert would be better off staying in Munich since he still had three years to go at the Luitpold, and besides, he spoke no Italian.

Before leaving, his parents made sure that he had a support system of relatives in place while they were gone, but in their absence, young Albert became more discontented with the school. He hadn't liked the Luitpold before, but now it was difficult for the young student to keep going. His letters to his family, however, didn't let on that anything was wrong. Six months after his parents had left for Italy, things came to a head for Albert.

One day, the Greek professor became aggravated with Albert, who protested that he hadn't done anything wrong. His professor agreed: "True, but you sit there in the back row smiling, and that violates the feeling of respect that a teacher needs from his class." He felt Albert's presence alone was enough to disrupt his class! The Greek professor wanted him to leave, but Albert may have already been planning his exit. He went to his family doctor and asked for a note that said he had a nervous disorder and needed to be on home rest. As part of his plan, Albert also approached his math professor and asked him for a letter of recommendation, which Albert received. On December 29, 1894, young Einstein turned in his medical note and was given permission to withdraw from the Luitpold. He would travel to Italy to be with his parents.

The Greek professor wanted him to leave, but Albert may have already been planning his exit.

CHAPTER 3

The Path to Higher Education

Thinking for its own sake, like music!

Albert was glad to end his time at the Luitpold but for reasons other than his dislike of the school. One incentive for leaving Germany was the law that said every German male had to perform military duty. In order to get out of this service, a young man would have to leave the country before he turned seventeen *and* give up his German citizenship. If he remained a citizen but left the country, he was then considered a "deserter."

At that time, the military was a very visible presence in Germany and a popular group among most children. But not to Albert. He had no intention of becoming a soldier. Even as a child, Albert disliked the "automaton," or robotic, look of the German soldiers. One day, when he was watching a military parade, someone told young Albert that he might march in one someday. Albert responded, "When I grow up I don't want to

Even though many children his age were fascinated by uniformed marching German soldiers, such as the ones shown in this 1896 photograph, Albert disliked the military.

be one of those poor people." Avoiding the army was one more reason the young German student chose to leave his homeland.

New Plans for the Future

Upon his dismissal from the Luitpold, Albert packed up and hopped a train for Italy. His parents were disappointed that he had dropped out of school, but he insisted that he had a plan and everything would be fine. His plan was to take the entrance exam to the Federal Polytechnic University in Zurich, Switzerland, in the fall.

The school did not require that students have a diploma to attend—they just had to pass the entrance exam. Although Albert was too young to attend, he got a special exemption by having a family friend assure the school that he was gifted, a "prodigy." He also had the letter of recommendation from the Luitpold math teacher. Albert promised to study for the exam beforehand, and since he had already declared that there was no way he'd go back to Munich, his parents agreed to let him try, despite their concerns.

Albert enjoyed being with his family and having the opportunity to do independent study. This was the first time he had traveled outside of the Munich area, and he found that the relaxed way of life in Italy agreed with him. He became more outgoing during this time and he would

Albert enjoyed his time with his family when he moved to Pavia, Italy, from Munich. This photograph of a cloister was taken in Pavia in the late 1800s.

later write of his "beautiful memories" of Italy.

While waiting to take the exam, Albert helped out at his uncle Jakob's design office on occasion. Jakob was impressed with his ability to provide fresh insight on challenging problems, and he said that his nephew would "go far one day." Albert did manage to get some studying done for the college exam also. His concentration was so focused, his sister wrote later, that he could work on a problem while sitting on the sofa surrounded by a large, noisy group of people.

One of the few concerns that troubled Albert during this time with his family was his father's ambition for him. Hermann wanted his son to work toward a technical profession, but Albert was much more interested in teaching math and physics. He preferred not to do something "practical." He just wanted to think about things. Explaining to a friend later, he said he enjoyed "thinking for its own sake, like music!"

> *He preferred not to do something "practical." He just wanted to think about things.*

Despite their differences, Albert's father helped him out on another matter. As his guardian, Hermann applied for his son's German citizenship to be revoked. Albert officially ceased to be a German national on January 28, 1896. For several years he went without having citizenship in any country, and when he filled out forms, he also wrote "no religious denomination." For now, Albert Einstein was a young man without a country or a religion.

In the summer of 1896, the Einstein brothers' company went bankrupt again. Rather than try to start another business, Jakob decided to work for someone else. But Hermann wanted to give it one more try. So he set up a new business in Pavia.

When it was time for Albert to take the Polytechnic entrance exam, he discovered that despite the considerable amount of private study he had done, he did not study all things equally. His entrance exam results were excellent in math and science, but too weak in other subjects for him to gain acceptance at the Polytechnic. Albert's parents were told that if he attended the final year of a Swiss secondary school, he could enter the Polytechnic the following year.

The Canton School in Aarau

Despite Albert's failure to gain entrance to the Polytechnic, the head of the school's physics department, Heinrich Weber, was very impressed with him, and the professor took the unusual step of inviting the young student to sit in on his lectures even before attending the Polytechnic. Unfortunately, Albert wasn't able to take Weber up on his offer because Albert moved to Aarau, Switzerland, for his last year of "high school" at the Canton School.

Einstein (seated far left) in his 1896 graduation photograph from Aarau suggests a confident young man.

In Aarau, Albert stayed with the Winteler family. The father, Jost Winteler, taught literature and history classes at the Canton School. He and his wife, Pauline, had seven children. Albert enjoyed the household so much and felt so at home that he called Jost and Pauline "Papa and Mama Winteler." Papa Winteler agreed with his boarder's feelings about German militarism and nationalism and predicted that there would be trouble in the future. Albert would comment later that Papa Winteler had been a very wise man.

Since leaving Germany, Albert had become more confident and sociable. Now, he was a handsome, flirtatious fellow with an irreverent streak. One member of the Winteler household who caught Albert's eye was Marie, their eighteen-year-old daughter. By Christmas, Albert and Marie were a couple, which pleased both the Wintelers and the Einsteins.

The atmosphere of the Canton School was very different from that of the Luitpold. Albert found that students were treated as individuals and encouraged to think for themselves. While he was there, he began pondering important physics questions such as: What would it be like to travel at the speed of light? What would he see if he were riding a wave of light? Albert would consider his questions to be "thought experiments," and he was capable of working on them for months or even years.

. . . he began pondering important physics questions such as: What would it be like to travel at the speed of light?

He enjoyed the school and successfully completed his studies in June 1896. To celebrate graduation, Albert and some classmates went on a three-day mountain hike, which proved to

Intertwined Relationships

Albert's life would always be intertwined with the Wintelers. In 1910, his sister, Maja, married Marie's brother, Paul, who thus became Albert's brother-in-law. But that wasn't the only family connection.

A man who would later become Albert's best friend married Marie's older sister, Anna. That man was Michelangelo ("Michele") Besso. Albert and Michele met in 1896, brought together by their shared love of classical music. They spent so much time discussing the special theory of relativity that Michele was one of the few people whom Albert thanked in his relativity paper.

World War II would separate Paul Winteler from his wife, Maja. Maja, who was Jewish, fled to the United States to escape Nazi persecution, and Paul remained in Europe. But Michele (and his relationship with Anna) would remain an inspiration for Albert until the end.

be a perilous trip. It was raining, and Albert slipped down a wet, slippery slope and headed toward a steep drop. Luckily, one of his classmates saw him and stretched out a walking stick for Albert to cling to while the rest of his friends pulled him to safety.

Albert and Marie Winteler were still seeing each other when he left for the Polytechnic in Zurich that September, but over the course of his first year, he called off their relationship. He didn't give her a reason, but it might have been because he had met the woman he would marry: a fellow student named Mileva Marić.

CHAPTER 4

Life at the Polytechnic

When a man sits with a pretty girl for one hour, it seems like a minute. But let him sit on a hot stove for a minute and it's longer than any hour. That's relativity.

During the first year at the Polytechnic, the emphasis was on mathematics and mechanics, but during his second year, Einstein got his first taste of real physics courses. Heinrich Weber, the physics department head who had been impressed with Einstein's entrance examination, taught Albert's first physics class. At first, the young student was thrilled. He came to class; he took notes; he thought Weber lectured "with great mastery." During the latter part of the year, however, Albert realized that Weber was not going to cover the more contemporary physics topics. Weber's interests lay in older physics theories. This

A c. 1900 photograph of the Polytechnic in Zurich, where Einstein attended his first physics class.

was unacceptable to Albert, and he stopped attending Weber's lectures and behaved disrespectfully toward the professor.

While at the Luitpold, Einstein had irritated a teacher by calling him by his last name rather than "Herr Professor," and he did the same thing with Heinrich Weber. "You are a very clever boy, Einstein, a clever boy, but you have one great fault: You never let yourself be told anything," Weber warned him. Smart as Einstein was, he should have realized that "Herr Weber" was not a person he should alienate.

As an independent thinker, Albert Einstein preferred to follow his own course.

As an independent thinker, Albert Einstein preferred to follow his own course. If he didn't want to attend a class, he didn't. If a class wasn't interesting to him, he preferred to study topics privately. But even a student as bright as Einstein had to conform to some school regulations. Luckily for him, his good friend Marcel Grossmann did not miss any classes and took thorough notes, which he willingly shared with Albert. Those notebooks saved Einstein's academic career.

Life Outside the Poly

Even though Einstein's class attendance was irregular, he kept busy by going to cafés with friends to discuss theories, problems, and experiments. A hot question of the day was, "How do you prove anything about aether?" Aether (or ether) was believed to be a weightless, invisible, and totally undetectable substance that carried light waves. Aether's relationship to light can be compared to waves in the ocean. Waves in the ocean are carried by water, and physicists believed light traveled in waves,

Aether

In 1887, Americans Albert Michelson and E. W. Morley did experiments to understand aether. They checked to see if light would travel more quickly "downstream" with the whoosh of the aether moving as the earth passes through it and more slowly "upstream" against this flow. Although they did very careful measurements, they weren't able to find any differences in the speed that light traveled.

Most scientists were puzzled by this result. But Einstein saw a solution: If there was no aether, and light travels at the same speed no matter which way it's traveling, there would be no difference in speed to detect.

too. They believed that aether—like water—carried light waves.

Physicists had been assuming that light waves from stars traveled on aether all the way to Earth, but no one had been able to prove the existence of aether. The aether question interested Einstein, and would turn out to be an important factor later on.

In addition to his stimulating café discussions, Einstein loved to pass the time playing his violin. During his third year at the Polytechnic, he hurt his hand in a physics experiment that had gone wrong. He needed stitches and was unable to play the violin for a while. "I greatly miss my old friend, through whom I say and sing to myself everything," he said. The loss was only temporary, and when his hand healed, Einstein was back on the strings. His violin not only gave him a creative outlet, it also helped him meet new people. In fact, it was at a home where musicians gathered to play on Saturday afternoons that Einstein met Michele Besso, who would become his lifelong friend.

A School Romance

It might be hard to imagine—if one has seen only pictures of Albert Einstein as an old man—but as a young man, Einstein was described by a female friend as having "the kind of male beauty that, especially at the beginning of the century, caused such havoc." He also played the violin masterfully, which women of all ages appreciated. Not only was Einstein a good-looking musician, he was a flirt. In later years he would explain the

While at the Polytechnic, the violin provided a creative outlet for Einstein. Even in his later years, he enjoyed playing his violin, as shown here in 1931.

theory of relativity this way: "When a man sits with a pretty girl for one hour, it seems like a minute. But let him sit on a hot stove for a minute and it's longer than any hour. That's relativity."

Kidding around or not, Albert Einstein always had an eye for the girls.

Not only was Einstein a good-looking musician, he was a flirt.

Although Einstein held women in high esteem, his opinion of men as romantic partners was low. He once said to a female friend who was worrying about a relationship, "Not too much should be expected from them, this I know quite exactly. Today we are sullen, tomorrow high-spirited, after tomorrow cold, then again irritated and half-sick of life—and so it goes—but I have almost forgotten the unfaithfulness and ingratitude and selfishness, things in which almost all of us do significantly better than the good girls."

At the Polytechnic, Albert Einstein met Mileva Marić, who was also attending the school. It was a small class of just five people, and Mileva was the only woman. At that time, Zurich was one of the only cities in Europe where a woman could get a university degree. Mileva was the fifth woman ever to attend the Polytechnic. She was born in 1875, in Vojvodina—an area of Hungary that would later become part of Yugoslavia—and was a few years older than Einstein. Mileva was **Serbian** and not Jewish—two facts that would annoy Einstein's parents when it became apparent that the young woman was important to their son.

Born with a dislocated hip, Mileva had a limp, a disability that made her parents fear that no one would ever want to marry her. She was a very smart child who showed an aptitude for math. The determined, serious side of her personality led her to be an

This photograph of a young Mileva Marić shows her as she was when she met Albert Einstein: determined, self-possessed, and serious.

excellent student, and the shy side prevented her from having any serious romantic experiences before she met Albert Einstein.

They became friends and, over the course of the year, developed a closer relationship. Mileva told her parents about her fondness for Albert Einstein, and over the summer, her father gave her some local tobacco to take to Einstein for his pipe when she saw him again at school. It was a kindness he would not have done had Einstein not been special to his daughter. But Mileva did not return to the Polytechnic with Einstein's tobacco. Instead, she headed to a different school, in Heidelberg, perhaps to put some distance between herself and the temptation of romance. After working so hard to get to college, she probably worried that marriage and children would distract her from the career she'd labored to secure.

Still, Mileva eventually returned to the Polytechnic after six months in Heidelberg, and she and Einstein soon took up where they had left off. Over time they studied together extensively and became very close. They even devised pet names for each other: Doxerl ("Dolly") and Johonzel ("Johnnie"). But after being away for so long in Heidelberg, Mileva had trouble getting back on track at the Polytechnic, and she wasn't able to graduate on time. Einstein, on the other hand, graduated with the rest of the class in July 1900, despite his independent ways.

After working so hard to get to college, she probably worried that marriage and children would distract her from the career she'd labored to secure.

Albert Einstein was now ready to go out and find a position, but having alienated his physics professor Heinrich Weber earlier on, he would discover that landing a job was no easy task.

Mileva and Albert met while studying at the Polytechnic and they quickly grew close. This photograph shows the couple in 1905, two years after they were married.

CHAPTER 5

Trying to Build a Future

I honored all the physicists from the North Sea to the southern tip of Italy with an offer of my services.

When twenty-one-year-old Albert Einstein graduated in the summer of 1900, he was qualified to teach math and science at secondary schools. Instead of a teaching job, however, his objective was to become an assistant to a Polytechnic professor while he wrote a **dissertation** to get an advanced degree. Einstein's other plan was to marry Mileva. Unfortunately for Einstein, obstacles stood in the way of both goals.

The first obstacle was at least partly of his own making: the miserable relationships he had with his teachers, especially Weber. Weber disliked Einstein so much that three days before exam time, he had him recopy an entire article because he had turned it in on "non-regulation" paper. After graduation, the other members of his four-person class were offered assistantships, but not Einstein.

Einstein's other dilemma was two-fold: His parents felt he couldn't "afford" a wife without a job. They also vigorously objected to the woman he'd chosen to marry. Einstein complained about the first part of the problem: that he needed money to have a wife. He argued that their attitude made a wife seem like a commodity that was being bought. But he said he went along with it, anyway, "to spare his parents."

While he accommodated his parents in that regard, he did not hide his intentions to marry Mileva. When his mother asked, "What will become of your little Dolly now?" upon hearing that Mileva had failed her exam, Einstein answered that she would become "my wife." His mother sobbed and grieved at this news. She felt Mileva would be an inattentive wife. And she didn't like that Mileva was Serbian (who were considered "gypsy" people), older than Albert, too independent as well as too intellectual, non-Jewish, and had a limp.

That year, Einstein spent the summer in Pavia with his parents, jobless and constantly arguing with them about Mileva. He relayed all of his mother's responses in detail to his fiancée. Mileva, who had been a determined and hard-working woman during the years before she attended the Polytechnic, became increasingly insecure as she heard how Einstein's mother viewed her. In Einstein's letters, mixed in with the stories about how

Albert's mother, Pauline Koch Einstein, was very much against a union between her son and Mileva Marić.

upset his parents felt about their relationship, were passionate statements like, "I'm so lucky to have found you, a creature who is my equal, and who is as strong and independent as I am! I feel alone with everyone except you."

Looking for Work

Although the atmosphere in the Einstein household was strained, Albert had an escape. Wherever he was and whatever he was doing, he always found time for private study. His ongoing thoughtful reading of the latest theories kept him stimulated and moving forward with his own ideas. He also enjoyed talking over his ideas with his good friend Michele Besso, who was living in Pavia with his wife and child. Besso would be an important sounding-board for Einstein over the years.

In August, Einstein returned to Zurich to look for an assistantship. Weber needed an assistant, but he could not bring himself to choose Albert Einstein. The irate professor decided that he would rather have non-physicists than that aggravating Einstein, who, for his part, might not have been willing to work with Weber, either. Jakob Ehrat, a college friend, recommended Albert for a life insurance position, but that wasn't the type of work Albert was looking for, either. All the while, Albert still pined for Mileva. He wrote to her, "How was I able to live alone

Albert loved to discuss his ideas with his friend Michele Besso, shown here with his wife, Anna Winteler, in 1898.

before I met you? Without you, I lack self-confidence, passion for work, enjoyment of life. In short, without you my life is no life."

Finally, Einstein decided that since he was not having much luck finding a job that he really wanted, he would return to Pavia and allow his father to teach him about the family business, which centered on electrical engineering projects. He also took on tutoring jobs.

Being Recognized as a Physicist

By December 1900, Einstein had finished writing a paper on capillarity (the interaction between a liquid meeting a solid) and it was accepted by the *Annalen der Physik* (Journal of Physics) for publication. The *Annalen der Physik* was the leading physics journal in Europe, so he and Mileva were very excited about the article being published. They felt as though he was finally starting to make some headway with his physics career. Einstein promised Mileva that they would spend Christmas together that

The *Annalen der Physik*

Albert's springboard to respectability was the *Annalen der Physik*, which was founded in 1790 by Friedrich Albert Carl Gren, a physics and chemistry professor at Halle University, in Germany. It was an important publication because it let the scientific community—including patent office workers—know about other physicists' experiments and theories.

The most famous writings the *Annalen der Physik* ever published were Einstein's papers in 1905, 1907, 1913, and 1916. Its most famous editor was Max Planck, who was associated with the journal for forty-eight years, from 1895 to 1943.

The journal was originally published in German, but today it is published in English. It is still ranked in the top ten of physics journals.

Annalen der Physik published many of Einstein's most famous papers, including his general theory of relativity (*Die Grundlage der allgemeinen Relativitats-theorie*) in 1916.

year, but when the time came, his parents talked him into spending Christmas in Pavia. They also gave him permission to finish his dissertation on the **kinetic** theory of gasses for the University of Zurich, but upon completion, they expected him to return to Pavia in the spring. Even though Einstein was almost twenty-two years old, he intended to comply with his parents' wishes.

Still looking for a position, Einstein sent letters to a number of professors in 1901, seeking an assistantship; he also included a copy of his capillarity paper. "I honored all the physicists from the North Sea to the southern tip of Italy with an offer of my services," he told Mileva. When no job offers were forthcoming, Einstein started to wonder why. Despite his intelligence, it hadn't occurred to him that Heinrich Weber's dislike of him would result in a negative **reference**.

He was frustrated with not having a job and afraid that he would not be able to succeed as a physicist.

Even though he received his Swiss citizenship on February 21, 1901, this period was a low point for Albert Einstein. He was frustrated with not having a job and afraid that he would not be able to succeed as a physicist. Not having a job meant that he was not able to marry Mileva or to help out his family. But things would soon start to look up. His friend Marcel Grossman had connections with the Swiss patent office in Bern, and he let Einstein know that there was an upcoming opening for a patent examiner there. Another friend also asked Einstein to teach a class for a couple of months. Einstein was excited to have two opportunities before him.

As husband and wife, Pierre and Marie Curie worked together in their laboratory and won the 1903 Nobel Prize in Physics. Mileva hoped that she and Albert could work together in the same way.

Einstein wasn't the only one with job possibilities. Mileva hoped to be hired for a teaching job in Croatia. Einstein wrote her, "If you don't get that position, and I get the job in Bern, I hereby appoint you my dear little scientist." Mileva had imagined that they would be like Pierre and Marie Curie—married scientists who would work together to make great discoveries.

An Unexpected Pregnancy

In May 1901, Einstein and Mileva met at Lake Como, in northern Italy, for a brief vacation. Even though they enjoyed their time away from their irate families and irritated professors, it was not too long afterward that Mileva realized she was pregnant. Although she was upset, Einstein was not too bothered by the news. To make things even more difficult for Mileva, she had to take her final examinations again while Einstein was off with his parents, who despised her. Upset and distracted, the young woman once again failed to pass her exams, which left her more upset and more dependent on Einstein than ever.

Although Einstein was pleased that things had started looking up for him in the spring, he was still not working steadily. He had the temporary teaching job, but the patent office job in Bern would not open up until the middle of 1902. His family's business had failed again, and his parents wanted him to help finance his sister's education. Financial pressures were weighing heavily on Einstein. In the summer of 1901, he told Mileva he would take the first job he could find, no matter how unrelated it was to what he wanted to do, so they could get married. Mileva certainly would have benefited from being able to relax during her pregnancy rather than worrying about the future, but instead, she encouraged him to wait for work that he really wanted to do.

In the fall, Einstein, who was living in Switzerland, found a temporary tutoring position that didn't pay much but was enough to keep him going for a while longer as a free spirit. As always, Einstein kept reading and thinking about physics. He read about an experiment that Philipp Lenard, Mileva's old Heidelberg teacher, had done with light. Metal contains charged particles called **electrons** (the particles that carry electricity). When light hits metal, these electrons can be knocked

Mileva's past teacher, physicist Philipp Lenard, won the 1905 Nobel Prize in Physics for his research on cathode rays, but in later years he would become known for his racist support of Nazism.

loose. This is known as **photoelectricity**. In Lenard's experiment the electrons in light always shot out at the same speed, whether he had used high or low light. The

As always, Einstein kept reading and thinking about physics.

intensity, or brightness, of light didn't affect the speed but its frequency—how closely packed the light waves were—did. Einstein thought this was *very* interesting. In a 1901 letter to Marcel Grossman, he wrote about how wonderful it felt to figure out something that was happening on a level that was "unconnected to the direct experience of the senses." Later, Einstein's interpretation of Lenard's experiment would become part of Einstein's theories that would turn the world upside down because they contradicted people's everyday experiences.

Moving to Bern and the Patent Office

In a November 1901 letter, Mileva refers to the baby she will have in two months by the name Lieserl (Little Lisa). Einstein was hoping they would have a boy, but Mileva dreamed of a daughter. By this time, Mileva had gone into hiding at her parents' house in Hungary to keep the Einsteins from finding out she was going to have a baby. Einstein's mother, Pauline, had already sent a

In June 1902, Albert Einstein started his job in the Bern patent office.

harsh letter to Mileva's parents that fall, saying hateful things about their daughter.

In December 1901, Einstein found out that the job with the patent office would definitely be his. He moved to Bern even though the job would not open up until the following June. A month later, at the end of January 1902, Mileva gave birth to a baby girl without Albert being there. She named her Lieserl, just as she had planned. The news of Lieserl's birth was communicated to Einstein in a letter from Mileva's father. The new father was enthusiastic. He wrote back that he loved the baby without even having seen her. His first letter to Mileva after Lieserl's birth was extraordinary because he never mentioned a word about science! But after that, Einstein still did not go and visit Mileva and Lieserl. In fact, there was no indication he ever met his daughter at all.

After his move to Bern, life was not going well for the budding genius: Einstein's apartment was seedy; he didn't have enough to eat; and didn't know what to do about his fiancée and daughter. But once he started work at the patent office in Bern in June of 1902, life became a little bit easier. Aside from providing a steady paycheck, his workplace offered Einstein other advantages.

Einstein and his fellow examiners checked out the patent submissions to see what would work and what wouldn't. As a result, a range of creative ideas came across his desk and provided Einstein with food for thought. In addition, when confusing patent descriptions were submitted, it was the job of the examiners to transform them into something understandable. Einstein enjoyed this challenge, which also provided good practice for his own scientific work.

As a result, a range of creative ideas came across his desk and provided Einstein with food for thought.

The atmosphere of the patent office was also a plus. Einstein liked his fellow examiners and the fact that he could walk to work. And when he was off duty, his time was all his own. He did not have to bring work home with him, and at times he was even able to do his own work at the office!

That October, Einstein went to Italy to see his father, who was dying of heart disease at the age of fifty-five. On his deathbed, Hermann gave Albert his permission to marry Mileva. Perhaps even though he was twenty-three and he was a father himself, Einstein was waiting for that permission to bring Mileva to Bern. Einstein felt guilty about his father's early death, blaming himself for not convincing his father to try a more stable business and for not being able to help him financially.

Albert and Mileva were finally married on January 6, 1903. The records about what happened to Lieserl are incomplete, but at this point, she had already either died or had been given up for adoption. Mileva was grieving the loss of the future she had imagined—with dual scientific careers and a baby daughter named Lieserl—but Einstein was about to enter an amazing moment in his professional life.

Albert and Mileva were eventually married and are shown here in Zurich in 1911.

CHAPTER 6

A Miracle Year

I've completely solved the problem.

While still working for the patent office, Einstein and his friends began meeting nightly to discuss theories and books they were reading. They called themselves "the **Olympia** Academy." One idea that held the Academy "spellbound for weeks" came from French mathematician Henri Poincaré, who wrote in 1902 that "there is no absolute time." Einstein was lucky to have friends who were interested by the same ideas that fascinated him. Despite Mileva's education and intelligence, she was not included in the academy, although she listened in on the nights that the group met at their home.

In June 1903, the couple took a belated honeymoon. That fall, Mileva told her husband that they would be having another child the following spring. Einstein was pleased by the news. Because times were tight, he applied for a promotion at the patent office but was declined. He needed to wait until he knew more about **mechanical engineering**.

On May 14, 1904, Hans Albert Einstein was born. Einstein tried to combine his studies with his fatherly

When Hans Albert was born in 1904, Einstein was a doting father to his infant first son.

duties. He would read while taking Hans Albert for a walk and would use the baby carriage as a movable desk.

Although Einstein enjoyed the high-level discussions he had with the Academy, he also wanted his good friend Michele Besso close enough to discuss ideas with him. He encouraged Besso to come work at the patent office, which he did at the end of 1904. Einstein loved to go over his questions about light with his close friend.

Ever since he was a teenager, Einstein had contemplated light. He had realized there was something strange about it. For example, when a person was in a car that was moving quickly and next to a car that was going the same speed, the person could look into the next car and see it basically "at rest." It was as if the speeds cancelled each other out. When Einstein imagined traveling as quickly as the speed of light, however, he realized that he could not envision light at rest. He kept wondering how light could be different from everything else.

He came to his conclusions not through experimentation but by reading and thinking.

In 1905, things came together for Albert Einstein in a phenomenal way. Even though he was working full-time at the patent office, he still found time to write groundbreaking articles. Even more amazing is the fact that Einstein did not have his own laboratory. He came to his conclusions not through experimentation but by reading and thinking. When he was once asked where his laboratory was, he held up his fountain pen.

Twenty-six-year-old Albert Einstein wrote one paper after another, and sent them all to the *Annalen der Physik*, the same science journal that had published his first paper on capillarity.

After a physicist had been published in their pages, the journal accepted all of the physicist's future submissions—even if they were unconventional.

Insights into Quantum Physics

In March, Einstein completed his paper on light. For two hundred years, scientists had thought light was a wave. The famed physicist Max Planck suggested in 1900 that light traveled through places and things in tiny packets or fixed units of energy, called quanta (from the Latin word for "how much"), rather than in waves. Einstein took the idea a step further, saying that light itself was made up of a stream of these quanta; light quanta are called photons. When scientists delved deeper into this idea, **quantum physics** was born.

Einstein described this photoelectricity paper as being "revolutionary." He was right. Many years later, his theory would help to create technology as diverse as lasers, transistors, cell phones, electron microscopes, DVD players, solar cells, weapons, cameras, aircraft, and magnetic resonance imaging (**MRI**).

Einstein's insights into photo-electricity led the way to higher technology today, including the electron microscope shown here being used in a laboratory in Germany.

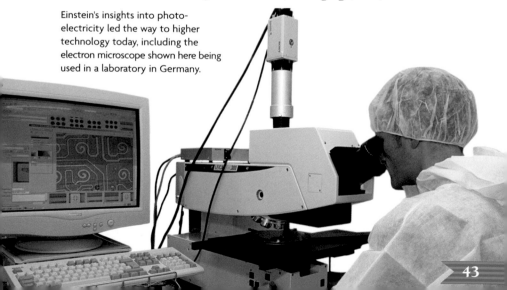

As time went on, Einstein would find the concepts of quantum physics deeply disturbing, however, and would spend many years opposing some aspects of the theory he had sparked. At this point, though, he was only answering questions; he wasn't considering what the impact of his answers would be.

Mileva continued to help Einstein with the mathematical aspects of his theories. She worked on the math at night after Hans Albert was in bed. Abraham Joffe, an *Annalen der Physik* editorial assistant, stated later that he saw two names signed on Einstein's first three 1905 papers: Einstein and Marity. Since Marity is the Hungarian version of Marić it would seem that, at first, Einstein gave Mileva official credit for assisting him with his work.

Focusing on Atoms

Einstein was aware that people often resisted believing that atoms existed because it was hard to imagine that all solid objects are actually made up of teeny particles in constant movement. Einstein used this topic as the subject for his University of Zurich dissertation.

At the end of April, Einstein finished "A New Determination of Molecular Dimensions" and submitted it to the University of Zurich. The first time he turned in the paper to the university, they told him it was too short.

This illustration depicts the structure of an atom. The center circle is a nucleus with smaller circles representing electrons moving around the nucleus. The paths of the electrons are shown as lines that form a flower-like pattern.

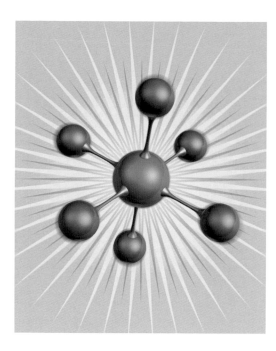

In this illustration an artist has depicted a model of a molecule.

After he added a sentence and turned it back in, however, they accepted it, to Einstein's amusement. He then sent this paper to the *Annalen der Physik* in August. In it, he showed a way to calculate the size of a molecule (thereby proving that molecules exist).

In May, Einstein submitted to the *Annalen der Physik* a paper on "Brownian motion." He said, "My major aim in this was to find facts which would guarantee as much as possible the existence of atoms of a definite, finite size." This work also supported the case that atoms are real, because in it Einstein showed how molecules move when they are heated. In the years to come, Einstein's 1905 Brownian motion paper would be referred to by scientists more than either his photoelectricity paper or his other famous work, his paper on special relativity.

Brownian Motion

In 1828, a scientist named Robert Brown looked at water under a microscope and noticed that even the purest water was packed with particles moving around like dust in sunlight. That movement became known as "Brownian motion," but no one could explain why that occurred—until Albert Einstein wrote about it in 1905. He calculated the average path a particle would take in a liquid or gas, after the particle was hit by a molecule. Einstein thought this path or trajectory might explain Brownian motion.

British botanist Robert Brown (1773–1858) was the first to notice the movement of particles in pure water, which became known as Brownian motion.

Realizing Special Relativity

That May, Einstein also had a breakthrough in his thinking about the problems of light, space, and time. The ideas of the seventeenth-century scientist Isaac Newton were the basis of physics at that time. Newton described how things move under the influence of visible forces—like hitting a ball with a bat—and invisible ones—like gravity. But Newtonian physics could not answer some of Einstein's questions. "It was as if the ground had been pulled out from under one, with no firm foundation to be seen anywhere," he said. It was up to him to create the new foundation, but it would not be done without a struggle. One evening in May, Einstein and his friend Michele Besso talked for hours on end about light, until finally Einstein despaired of ever finding the answers.

Isaac Newton

In England, in 1642, a child was born who would turn out to be one of the most remarkable mathematicians and scientists who ever lived. His name was Isaac Newton. He laid out universal rules for scientific study, figured out the mathematics of **orbits**, co-invented calculus and, in 1687, he wrote a book, *Philosophiae Naturalis Principia Mathematica* (*Mathematical Principles of Natural Philosophy*), whose title is often referred to as the *Principia*.

The Principia state Newton's three laws, which are:

1. An object remains at rest or in uniform motion unless acted upon by an external force (the law of inertia).

2. For a constant mass, force equals mass times acceleration: $F = ma$. (When a force is applied to an object, it accelerates.)

3. For every action, there is an equal and opposite reaction.

In Westminster Abbey in London a Latin inscription sums up the feelings people had about Newton: "Mortals, rejoice that there has existed so great an ornament to the human race!"

This undated engraving depicts Isaac Newton conducting light experiments.

When he saw Michele the next day, however, Einstein announced, "Thank you. I've completely solved the problem." What had proved so elusive the night before had somehow come within reach while he had slept. This new insight gripped Einstein, and he spent every possible moment writing out his conclusions. He ended up with a thirty-one-page paper, which he titled "On the Electrodynamics of Moving Bodies." Einstein didn't mention the phrase "theory of relativity" in the paper, but later it would be referred to, by Max Planck and others, as the special theory of relativity. Einstein, however, actually preferred Hermann Minkowski's 1908 description of it as the theory of "invariant postulates." Perhaps "relativity" was easier to remember in the public's mind.

Einstein's theory of special relativity boldly presented a new way of looking at the world. The fact that it didn't match the way people experienced their everyday lives made it daring for Einstein to suggest it in the first place and difficult for most people, even physicists, to understand.

What had proved so elusive the night before had somehow come within reach while he had slept.

Most physicists had assumed that time and space were always the same and that everyone experienced them to be the same, although Galileo had pointed out that a person on a moving ship watching another ship standing still might think he was standing still and the other ship moving. Still, physicists assumed that however things might appear, a second is a second is a second, and an inch is an inch is an inch, no matter where you are or whether you are moving or still. They thought that the thing that *was* changeable was light. Just as a car appears to move faster to someone standing on the side of the road than to someone driving in the same direction, a beam of light leaving a flashlight was expected to look faster to someone holding the flashlight than it would to someone running in the same direction as the beam of light.

Einstein, however, showed that, in a vacuum (where there is no air or other matter to interfere), the speed of light always remains the same (186,282 miles per second or 299,792,458 meters per second) no matter how slowly or quickly the person measuring it moves, and he made the startling insight that as something approaches that speed, it is actually space and time that look different to people in different states of motion, and the fast-moving object will experience time and space differently than slower ones do. He was able to demonstrate his ideas using mathematics.

In everyday life, nothing else goes anywhere near the speed of light. No one runs, drives, or flies that fast. As a result, the changes Einstein predicted aren't noticeable to us. However, electrons, the atomic particles that carry electrical charge, can move at speeds approaching the speed of light, and out in space, other galaxies may be traveling at similar speeds. As a result, special relativity applies to processes that are taking place at **microscopic** and **macroscopic** levels.

After finishing the paper—his fourth submission to *Annalen der Physik* that year, not including the numerous summaries of scientific papers he'd been writing on the side—Einstein took to his bed for several days.

Although he hadn't cited any other scientists in his paper, Einstein felt philosopher David Hume and physicist-philosopher Ernst Mach had been significant

Einstein cited philosopher David Hume as the inspiration for his theory on special relativity.

An Example of Special Relativity

As an example of special relativity, imagine an experiment with two perfectly synchronized **atomic clocks**. If one clock was placed on an airplane that could travel around the globe at light speed while the other clock was left at the airport, when the plane returned, the clocks would not tell the same time. The clock on the plane would show that a shorter amount of time had passed compared with the amount of time shown on the clock on the ground. Similarly, the pilot on the plane and a person with the clock on the ground would have experienced the passage of different amounts of time.

Have different amounts of time actually passed? It's all relative. A person in a car traveling alongside a fast-moving train may say the train isn't going very fast because he can easily watch the passengers in the train, while a person standing on the sidewalk watching the same train zip by will believe it was going much too fast for the passengers to be more than blurs. Einstein's theory shows that, for objects moving very, very fast, there is a measurable difference in space and time.

The idea that time is variable has inspired many writers to create fictional time machines.

About a decade after H. G. Wells's classic novel *The Time Machine* was published, Einstein furnished the scientific foundation for the time travel.

inspirations for his discovery. Ernst Mach had rejected the notion that time and space were absolute (independent and unchanging), because that couldn't be proved by our senses. Einstein's special relativity theory says that time and space are not absolute, but different for different observers. David Hume's philosophy, which encouraged thinking in new ways rather than just established ones, helped encourage Einstein to oppose Isaac Newton's theories. He did also add a note at the end thanking Michele Besso.

Mileva, Hans, and Einstein went to Serbia in August to visit family and friends. For Mileva, this visit—with her solidly employed husband and toddler son—was a far cry from the miserable time she had spent there waiting for Lieserl to be born. Proudly, she told her father, "Not long ago we finished a very significant work that will make my husband world famous." Mileva would prove to be right about that.

The Most Famous Equation

Although Einstein was finished with his special relativity paper, he continued thinking about it. He wound up writing a three-page addition to his paper and sending it along to the *Annalen der Physik* in September. This new work was called "Does the Inertia of a Body Depend on Its Energy Content?" and, though he didn't write it out as such in the paper, the ideas he discussed would give us the world's most famous equation: $E = mc^2$.

In 1907, Einstein was asked to write about his special relativity theory. In this paper, he first wrote the equation $E = mc^2$. He concluded that everything in the universe contains gigantic amounts of potential energy (energy due to its mass alone). His equation was not investigated experimentally for twenty-five years because scientists didn't have the equipment to check if he was right. Technology had to catch up with Albert Einstein.

British physicist John Cockcroft and Irish physicist Ernest T. S. Walton provided the first experimental evidence of $E = mc^2$ in 1932, when they developed the first **nuclear particle accelerator**. Their work showed that energy and mass were the same. They won the Nobel Prize for their work in 1951.

What Does $E = mc^2$ Mean?

Understanding the equation $E = mc^2$ requires a basic understanding of each part of the equation. Simply defined, **E** stands for "energy," which is the ability to do work and overcome any opposition or resistance, and **m** represents "mass," which is a unit of measurement that describes how much matter is in an object, or how much space that object takes up. Finally, **c** refers to the speed of light. The letter "c" is used to represent the speed of light because it stands for *celeritas*, the Latin word for "swiftness." Therefore, when written out, the equation reads: Energy equals mass times the speed of light squared (multiplied by itself).

But what does this mean? Put simply, that energy and mass are fundamentally the same thing, and you can figure out how much of each is associated with the other by using this equation. Mass approaching the speed of light becomes equivalent to energy, and energy slowed down becomes massive. Mass seems solid, and energy is not—so picturing them as interchangeable is not the easiest thing to do.

Einstein's formula is so recognizable, it is often seen in pop art. In this photo, Germany presented $E = mc^2$ on a grand scale in May 2006, in the form of this sculpture at the Altes Museum in Berlin.

CHAPTER 7

From Place to Place

I believe in [Baruch] Spinoza's God, Who reveals Himself in the lawful harmony of the world, not in a God Who concerns Himself with the fate and the doings of mankind.

Although Einstein had written some remarkable papers in 1905, he was still a young unknown working in the patent office. But it didn't take long for his work to draw the attention of Europe's most famous physicist, Max Planck. Einstein was pleased that the great scientist was interested in his papers and he was happy to discuss them with Planck and answer questions about them. Planck was particularly interested in special relativity, but he had some issues with the photoelectricity paper. Although he himself had suggested earlier that light was sometimes quanta, Planck thought Einstein was going too far by saying that light was always quanta.

In April 1906, Albert Einstein was promoted to "Technical Expert Second Class" and he received a raise. Between the patent office and his

Albert was pleased when the Nobel Prize–winning German physicist Max Planck, photographed here in 1918, expressed interest in a number of Einstein's theories.

own work, Einstein carried a staggering workload. Between 1905 and 1909, he published more than two dozen papers explaining aspects of relativity and answering criticisms of it, while also writing papers on other related topics.

In addition to writing more papers, he was also spending a lot of time responding to letters from other scientists. Einstein followed the customary practice of sending his photo with letters to other physicists. The photo he sent shows a stylishly dressed young man—very different from the messy-looking Albert Einstein of his later years!

Einstein's Olympia Academy wasn't meeting anymore because the other members had left town, so he tried to get more friends to move to Bern. He wasn't able to convince anyone to come, but he still saw Michele Besso on Sundays when Michele and his wife would visit. Maja, Einstein's sister, also came over on Sundays. She was attending Bern University, working on her PhD in Romance languages.

During the summer of 1907, Einstein's thoughts took a turn toward inventing. While on vacation, he got an idea for a machine that would measure tiny amounts of energy, which would allow him to confirm his Brownian motion theory. He made a drawing of it and sent it to his friends Conrad and Paul Habicht for construction. The Habicht brothers built a machine based on the drawing, and Einstein and Mileva worked to perfect it. Einstein was

As a young man, Albert Einstein took care to present himself as neat and stylish, as seen in this 1910 photograph.

Albert's beloved "Olympia Academy," made up of his intellectual friends, provided an informal forum for discussing new and exciting ideas. From left to right: Paul Habicht, Maurice Solovine, and Albert Einstein, c. 1910.

excited about the *Maschinchen* ("little machine"), but manufacturers were not very interested. Paul Habicht manufactured it himself for twenty years; however Einstein lost his enthusiasm for it around 1911.

While the machine didn't work out for Einstein the way he had hoped, inventiveness came in handy for him at home. A strong memory from his son's childhood was of his father constructing a cable car out of matchboxes and string. The young Hans Albert thought it was beautiful.

Breaking into the Academic World

The patent office had been a comfortable job when Einstein first started working there, but in 1907, he decided he wanted to get into the academic world. In June, he applied to Bern University to become an unsalaried lecturer, which was the first step to becoming a professor. Part of the application requirement was to turn in an unpublished paper, but because Einstein didn't have any at that moment, he turned in seventeen published papers instead. The physics department was unimpressed and turned him down for the lack of an unpublished paper. Aime Forster, the department head, also complained that his theory of special relativity was impossible to understand.

Einstein still wasn't finished with relativity. His special theory of relativity only applies to things moving at *constant* speeds. At a constant speed, how fast something is going can only be determined *in relation* to something else. But Einstein also was interested in *inconstant* speeds (changing speed created through acceleration and inertia). Why did things resist being moved? How could gravity be included in his theory?

One day at the patent office, Einstein had a revelation: A person in free fall will not feel his or her own weight. The concepts that sparked from this realization made him later call this "the happiest thought of his life." What makes it possible to not feel your own weight when falling is that every molecule in the body accelerates at the exact same rate. If different parts of a falling body traveled at different speeds, falling would be a different thing entirely! But gravity acts on all objects completely equally. People had known that to be true since philosopher, astronomer, and mathematician Galileo's discoveries in the fifteenth century, but no one had explained the reason.

One day at the patent office, Einstein had a revelation: A person in free fall will not feel his or her own weight.

Since every molecule is acted upon equally, a person falling down a mile-long elevator, for instance, wouldn't be able to feel gravity. The person could think that he or she was staying still and that the surroundings were going up. Thinking about it that way made gravity seem relative to Einstein. Plus, he saw that gravity acted on a body the same way that acceleration did: There was the same pull.

He started considering inertial mass (the resistance of a body to being moved) and gravitational mass (how strongly gravity tugs on a body) in the same way. This sameness is known as "the principle of equivalence." This principle means that the effects of standing on Earth and accelerating at roughly 9.8 meters per second squared (the value of the Earth's gravitational field) are equal.

It would take Einstein eight more years to completely understand gravity—but when he was done, he would have completed the general theory of relativity! It took an especially long time because the mathematical equations that went along with the theory were extremely difficult.

Bern University

Not one to give up easily, Einstein tried again in February 1908 to secure a lecturing position at Bern University. This time he submitted an unpublished paper, and he was accepted. On the day of his first lecture, which was scheduled for 7 a.m., only three people attended. One of the three audience members was his friend Michele Besso, who couldn't help but notice that the new speaker was nervous and unprepared. For all of his knowledge, Einstein really didn't know how to give lectures.

At one point, Maja, Einstein's sister, came to watch him, and

On the day of his first lecture, which was scheduled for 7 a.m., only three people attended.

she noticed that his appearance was starting to suffer. She blamed this change on his preoccupation with his work. He was essentially doing two jobs—one at the patent office and one as a lecturing physicist—which she felt was overtaxing her brother. But Maja wasn't the only one to make this observation about his heavy workload. Jakob Laub, a math student who would become Einstein's first collaborator, wrote to Einstein, saying, "I must tell you frankly that I was surprised to read that you must sit in an office for eight hours a day. History is full of bad jokes." Physicist–political activist Friedrich Adler also commented to his father, the politician Victor Adler, in 1908, ". . . it is felt to be a scandal not only here but also in Germany that a man like that should sit in the patent office."

Although the special theory of relativity was gaining some supporters, other scientists were resisting the theory that light traveled as a stream of particles. Einstein was so fascinated by the "quantum question" that he wrote it was "so incredibly important and difficult that everyone should busy themselves on it." His goal was to figure out the mathematics to show that light was both wave *and* particles (quanta).

The University of Zurich

In 1909, a spot opened up at the University of Zurich, in the physics department. If Einstein could secure this position, it would be a paying position for him, unlike the unpaid work at Bern University. His greatest competition for the job was Friedrich Adler, but Adler recommended Einstein, saying he was the better physicist. However, when the department head came to see him lecture in Bern, things went badly. The department head was displeased to see a disheveled young physicist talking over the head of his one and only student.

The Physics Institute of the Swiss Federal Institute of Technology (ETH), where Einstein secured a paid teaching position.

After that less than stellar showing, Einstein asked for another chance to try, and the department head let him "audition" at the Zurich Physical Society. Afterward, Einstein stated, "Contrary to my habit, I lectured well on this occasion." This time, the young physicist was hired. Einstein and Mileva had lived in seven different places during the seven years he had worked for the patent office, and now the family of three was moving to Zurich! Einstein resigned from the patent office on July 6, 1909.

Einstein, Mileva, and Hans Albert moved into an apartment building in Zurich, where Hans Albert found a downstairs playmate in their building: Friedrich Adler's daughter, Assinka. In a happy coincidence, Adler and his family lived in the same building as the Einsteins. Although Friedrich hadn't taken Einstein's job, he was still a university lecturer as well as the editor of a local political newspaper.

Being back in Zurich was pleasant for the couple, and Mileva became pregnant again. Nonetheless, the relationship between Mileva and Einstein was strained. In the fall, a difficult situation arose when Einstein got back in touch with an old female friend,

Anna Meyer-Schmid. Mileva saw what she considered to be an inappropriate letter from Anna to Einstein, and she wrote Anna, telling her to leave Einstein alone. Anna's husband also saw Mileva's letter. Einstein was embarrassed about the whole thing and irritated with his wife.

> *Although Mileva cared deeply for Einstein, this incident showed that Einstein probably had eyes for other women.*

Although Mileva cared deeply for Einstein, this incident showed that Einstein probably had eyes for other women and wasn't really interested in improving his relationship with his wife. Instead, Einstein would rather distance himself from her, and he found this easier to do by having other people around all the time. Teaching was not something that Einstein kept in the classroom. He would bring students back to the apartment, go with them to cafés, and take them hiking. Anywhere was a good place for talking about physics, and Einstein loved to talk. His enthusiasm and willingness to treat them as equals made him a favorite professor among students.

Enough attention now was being drawn to Einstein's theories, and in 1909 he received his first Nobel Prize nomination. He didn't win, but he would continue to be nominated for seven out of the next nine years. Ironically, one of the people who nominated Einstein in 1910 was someone who had turned him down when he'd applied for an assistantship in 1901. How things had changed in less than a decade!

The German University

Six months after arriving in Zurich, Einstein was invited to apply to the German University in Prague, the capital of Bohemia in the Austria-Hungarian Empire. Mileva was against the move because she liked living in Zurich. Einstein's students also wanted him to stay and campaigned to get him a better situation in Zurich. At first the professorship at Prague was offered to someone else. However, the gentleman asked for too much money, so the German University turned to Einstein, who agreed to come to Prague the following spring. But there was a certain amount of red tape the Einsteins had to go through first. For one thing, at Zurich, Einstein had identified himself as nonreligious. Now, he was required to declare his religion for Prague, so he called himself "a Jew of the **Mosaic** religion."

On July 28, 1910, Mileva gave birth to their second son, Eduard. Eduard and Mileva were slow to recuperate from the birth, but once Mileva recovered, she had to care for her new baby and Hans Albert as well as plan for another move—one she was reluctant to make. The relationship between Germans and **Slavs** was typically not a very friendly one, so as a Serbian Slav, Mileva was not looking forward to going to the German University.

Einstein and his family arrived in Prague on April 1, 1911. This was the first job where Einstein was welcomed as a celebrity. But even as "celebrities" they had to put up with less than ideal conditions in their new home, including dirty water, bedbugs, and fleas. Still, Einstein's favorite thing about the new university was its library. He also enjoyed playing his violin and performing with other musicians. Music would be a constant in his

Even as "celebrities" they had to put up with less than ideal conditions in their new home, including dirty water, bedbugs, and fleas.

The Nobel Prize

When Alfred Nobel died in 1896, he left behind instructions to create prizes for people who made special contributions to humanity in the fields of physics, chemistry, medicine or physiology, literature, and peace. The first Nobel Prizes were awarded five years later, in 1901.

Alfred Nobel was born in 1833, in Stockholm, Sweden. He became a scientist and an inventor. When Nobel was thirty-three years old, he invented dynamite, which he patented the following year. Covering all his bases, Nobel also patented a blasting cap, which was a way to ignite the dynamite by lighting a fuse. These inventions were popular for construction work, such as blowing up rocks and excavating tunnels. Nobel built factories in more than twenty countries. He traveled around, visited his factories, and kept on inventing. When he died, Nobel held 355 patents.

The front and back of Einstein's Nobel Prize medal..

One thing he did not have, though, was a family of his own. When Alfred Nobel was trying to decide what to do with all the money he was making with his patents and factories, he imagined a prize for exceptional achievements in service to humankind. Since the Nobel Prize was founded, nearly eight hundred prizes have been awarded.

nomadic life, and he was good enough to receive this "review" years later from a music critic who didn't realize Einstein was a physicist: "Einstein's playing is excellent, but he does not deserve his world fame; there are many others just as good."

One of the funniest Einstein-related music stories comes from pianist Artur Schnabel. Schnabel was playing in a quartet with Einstein, who kept coming in at the wrong time. Frustrated, Schnabel finally said, "For

When Einstein arrived in Prague to teach at the German University, he was hailed as somewhat of a teaching celebrity. This photograph of the Old Town Square in Prague was taken sometime between 1890 and 1905.

heaven's sake, Einstein, can't you *count*?" Even a man who is regarded as a genius had trouble getting it right sometimes.

Trying to Prove Relativity

Just as with his trips from one university to another, Einstein was moving back and forth between quantum theory and the theory of relativity. In 1910, other scientists' experiments confirmed predictions Einstein had made based on quantum theory. It was very exciting for him to know that he was on the right track. Now in Prague, he decided to go back to relativity. Einstein had taken a break from figuring out how to include gravity in relativity when he realized that the impact of the earth's gravity on something like light beams was too small for him to measure. Considering the problem again later, he realized that the sun was big enough to have a measurable impact.

Throughout his life, Albert Einstein enjoyed playing the violin. He is shown here with a pianist and a cellist in 1933.

A consequence of the sun's more powerful gravity, Einstein concluded, would be that starlight passing the sun would be bent on its way to the earth. The problem was, the sun was generally too bright for starlight passing near it to be visible. During a solar **eclipse**, starlight next to the sun would be more visible, and his theory could be proven. Einstein published a paper called "On the Influence of Gravitation on the Propagation of Light," which encouraged astronomers to try it.

Einstein also thought of other ways his ideas about gravity could be proved. His theory of relativity said that light passing through a **gravitational field** will slow down. When it slows down, light's wavelength gets longer, so the light shifts toward the red end of the **spectrum**, so Einstein thought that the sun would show an example of the "redshift." To test this, light radiated from atoms in the sun could be compared with light from similar atoms on Earth. If relativity theory was correct, the sun's atoms would have a longer wavelength (it would be redder).

He also thought the theory of relativity could be used to explain Mercury's **elliptical** orbit. Mercury is the planet nearest to the sun, and each time it reaches its closest point to the sun in its path around it, it shifts a little bit forward (closer to the sun). Einstein's theory predicted this shift more accurately than Newton's did. Astronomers and mathematicians would use his suggestions to evaluate his theory.

In August 1911, Einstein came down with a stomach ailment—a condition that would cause difficulties for him

The Solvay Conference

The Solvay Conference was founded by Ernest Solvay, of Belgium. Like Alfred Nobel, Ernest Solvay was a scientist who became wealthy through his work and decided to use his money for civic-minded causes. Unlike Nobel, Solvay began his good works within his own lifetime. He founded schools, became a senator, and was even appointed minister of state, as well as established the Solvay Conference for physics.

Even today, the Solvay Conference continues to be held every three years to promote the best in physics research.

The Solvay Conference attracted world-class physicists from around the globe. Einstein (standing second from right) attended the 1911 conference in Brussels, Belgium, along with Marie Curie (seated second from right).

throughout his life. By October, he was well enough to attend the first Solvay Conference in Brussels, Belgium. The Solvay Conference was the first world physics conference, and it was attended by invitation only.

Out of the twenty-four physicists at the Solvay Conference, eight would become or were already Nobel Prize winners. Although Einstein was the youngest person there, he impressed the others. Dutch physicist Hendrik Lorentz acted as the chairperson of the event. Einstein told his friend Heinrich Zangger that Hendrik Lorentz was "a living work of art!" He also enjoyed meeting other attendees including Max Planck and Marie Curie.

A Marriage on the Rocks

In early 1912, the ETH (Swiss Federal Institute of Technology), in Zurich, offered Einstein a full professorship and an increase in salary. He also received offers from Austria, Germany, and the Netherlands, but he settled on Switzerland, a decision that pleased his entire family. "Great joy about it among us all and the two bear cubs," he said, referring to his sons as the "cubs."

Before the family left Prague in July of 1912, Einstein visited Berlin in the spring. While there, he visited his cousin Elsa Löwenthal, whom he had not seen since they were children. Elsa, who was three years older than Einstein, had recently been divorced and had two young children, Ilse and Margot. After his visit, the pair started corresponding in secret. Elsa wrote Einstein only at his office and asked him to destroy the letters after he read them. Einstein told her that he found Mileva unlikable. "I have to have someone to love, otherwise life is miserable. And that someone is you. . . ." Einstein waffled about is relationship with Elsa as he wrote to her, "If we give in to our affection for each other, only confusion and misfortune will result."

Nevertheless, the Einstein family celebrated their return to Zurich with a day in the mountains. Hans Albert and his father hiked the glaciers while Mileva and Tete (Eduard's nickname) picked mushrooms. But things would not go well for Einstein and Mileva. She was still unhappy even though they had left Prague. Mileva never wanted her marriage to Einstein to come to an end, but his feelings toward her had soured.

Back at the ETH, Einstein was with his old friend Marcel Grossman, the mathematician. They started working on Einstein's questions and theories about gravity together, with Grossman handling the mathematics and Einstein doing the theorizing.

Working on relativity became all-consuming for Einstein.

Hans Albert wondered about his father's work and asked him: "Father, we are quite alone, nobody can see or hear us. Now you can tell me frankly—is this relativity story all bunk?" Einstein loved his question.

Working on relativity became all-consuming for Einstein. He wrote, "In all my life I have not labored nearly so hard, and I have become imbued with great respect for mathematics. . . . Compared with this problem, the original relativity is child's play." Einstein said he was trying to "know God's thoughts." He talked a lot over the years about God. He said, "I believe in [Baruch] Spinoza's God, Who reveals Himself in the lawful harmony of the world, not in a God Who concerns Himself with the fate and doings of mankind."

Grossman and Einstein published a paper called"Generalized Theory of Relativity and a Theory of Gravitation" in 1913, but they hadn't gotten the science quite right. They had worked hard to come up with the theory, but they had more work ahead.

CHAPTER 8

Gaining Notoriety

The gentlemen in Berlin are gambling on me as if I were a prize hen. As for myself, I don't even know whether I'm going to lay another egg.

When Albert Einstein turned thirty-four, in March 1913, he received a birthday card from his cousin Elsa. Their correspondence began again. "I treat my wife as an employee whom I cannot fire," he told her. That summer, Einstein would receive an offer to move to Berlin. He saw this as an opportunity to be close to Elsa. But beyond his romantic relationship, what would make him want to move back to a place where he had given up his citizenship and was, in his opinion, a less than desirable place to live? The answer was: a sweet offer.

In the summer of 1913, Einstein's friends Max Planck and Walther Nernst came to Zurich to try to convince him to come to Berlin. They told him he could be the director of the Kaiser Wilhelm Institute for Physics in Berlin, once the institute was set up. He would be part of the Prussian Academy of Sciences. He would have a professorship at Friedrich-Wilhelm University, where he could lecture as much or as little as he wanted. In

He told them that, upon their return, if he greeted them with red flowers in his hand, that would mean he would accept their offer.

other words, Einstein could focus on research in a place where more scientists were interested in relativity than anywhere else, and he would also be paid very well.

Einstein told Max and Walther that he needed to think about it, so the two of them went sightseeing for a few days while he thought it over. He told them that, upon their return, if he greeted them with red flowers in his hand, that would mean he would accept their offer. If he was carrying white flowers, that would mean he would decline. They were relieved to see Einstein greet them with red flowers in his hand. He told a friend later, "The

Colleagues for many years, Max Planck and Einstein are shown talking at the second World Power Conference in June 1930. At this convention of energy experts, Einstein spoke about his theory of the reality of space.

gentlemen in Berlin are gambling on me as if I were a prize hen. As for myself, I don't even know whether I'm going to lay another egg." He would stay in Zurich until April 1914 —arriving in Germany a few months before World War I would begin.

Life on His Own

It wasn't long before Mileva and the children left Berlin to go back to Zurich. Living together wasn't very rewarding for either Albert or Mileva, and it felt completely impossible to Mileva to stay in Berlin—under the hostile eye of Einstein's family—while she and her husband were not getting along. Michele Besso, ever the helpful friend, came to Berlin that summer to escort Tete, Hans Albert, and Mileva back to Switzerland. Hans Albert later said that his parents split up because his father didn't want anything to distract him from his work.

Hans Albert later said that his parents split up because his father didn't want anything to distract him from his work.

That might not have been accurate, but his concentration was great enough that social niceties were lost on him. For instance, one evening at astronomer Erwin Freundlich's house, Einstein began writing all over their party tablecloth because he wanted to show some equations. On another occasion, someone teased Einstein by saying that if he were actually in love, he would find that more important than quantum theory. Einstein disagreed, saying that his quantum theories were very dear to him.

Einstein was sad to see his children go, but he had an exciting event on his mind: an upcoming eclipse. This eclipse would provide an opportunity to see if starlight really bent around the sun. In anticipation of the event, Erwin Freundlich arranged to go to Russia to see the eclipse and take photographs.

When Germany declared war on Russia on August 1, 1914, Freundlich was there, preparing for the eclipse. Einstein worried for his safety. As it turned out, Freundlich was arrested and his equipment was taken, but he was sent back to Berlin in an exchange for Russian prisoners of war. The proof Einstein had been looking for would have to wait.

Taking a Stand on War

The war drove Einstein to join his first political party in November 1914: *Bund Neues Vaterland* (New Fatherland League). Not only did he join the party, he was one of its founding members. Goals of the group included an early peace and the creation of an international organization that would prevent future wars. They took risks, smuggling letters and books into prisons. It was not too surprising that in a country that tolerated little opposition, the New Fatherland League would be outlawed in February 1916.

Einstein wrote to a friend that if there were an island somewhere for people who were kind and sensible, "there I too would be a fervent patriot." He might have wished to be somewhere different, but he made do with his actual situation fairly well. Elsa lived near his apartment, so he could seek out companionship and home-cooked meals easily. He said that their relationship would last because of "the avoidance of matrimony." Einstein, who felt he did not have legal cause to divorce Mileva, sent her money regularly. The amount wasn't enough to cover the rent, so she gave math and piano lessons to supplement it.

Elsa lived near his apartment, so he could seek out companionship and home-cooked meals easily.

Manifestos on the War

Most of Einstein's colleagues supported the war enthusiastically. Ninety-three scientists, poets, painters, and other intellectuals signed the "Manifesto to the Civilized World," released in October of 1914. The manifesto—a public declaration of intentions—insisted that the world should not be upset with Germany for invading Belgium, even though it was a neutral country, because Germany was just protecting itself from "Russian hordes." They claimed that German soldiers didn't harm any Belgian citizens or their property. This statement was an obvious lie, and, for many reasons, "the civilized world" was unmoved by the manifesto. Einstein was also disappointed by the manifesto's false claims, particularly since so many of his colleagues, including Max Planck, had signed it.

Einstein signed a counter-manifesto, written by University of Berlin physiology professor Georg Nicolai. Einstein might have had a hand in writing it as well. This document, titled a "Manifesto to the Europeans," called for peace and a united Europe. It was circulated among Berlin intellectuals, but only four—including Nicolai and Einstein—signed it. One of the four was even someone who had signed the previous manifesto! It was brave to write it and brave to sign it, but they found it was not an effective tool. Nicolai's career actually suffered for it, but Einstein was given some license because he was officially a Swiss citizen.

Ironically, the money that supported Einstein and his family came from people who embraced the war he opposed. One of them was a pro-war colleague named Fritz Haber, who wanted to help the war cause so much that he pioneered chemical warfare.

His first experiment was about 160 tons of chlorine blown over French troops in Belgium in April 1915. Although it was a breach of the Hague Convention of 1907, Germany continued its program of chemical warfare, with Haber as its director.

Nevertheless, the fact that Einstein was alone in his antiwar feelings didn't seem overly bothersome to him for he was busy with work. One day, the astronomer Erwin Freundlich came to see him and noticed he had a unique mail-filing system. There was a meat hook hanging from the ceiling with a stack of letters stuck to it. Einstein explained he didn't have time to reply to them. When Erwin asked him what he did when the hook was full, Einstein answered, "Burn them."

A youthful-looking Einstein is shown walking in Germany in 1920.

The General Theory of Relativity

The work that preoccupied Einstein was his general theory of relativity. In November 1915, his hard work paid off. Einstein finally got to the bottom of his problems with the general theory of relativity equations and successfully combined gravity with space, time, matter, and energy. "The theory is beautiful beyond comparison," he commented.

In the summer of 1915, Einstein lectured on general relativity at Göttingen, Germany, saying afterward, "To my great joy, I completely succeeded in convincing [David] Hilbert and [Felix] Klein." Following his lecture, Einstein and mathematician

David Hilbert continued a discussion of Einstein's theory. Hilbert was so convinced that Einstein was correct in his theory that Hilbert submitted a paper for publication that included the general relativity equations six days before Einstein publicly presented the equations. Einstein was afraid he was being plagiarized, but Hilbert acknowledged that Einstein was the originator of the theory.

After the *Annalen der Physik* published Einstein's article detailing the general theory, he sent a copy to Willem de Sitter, a Dutch

Albert Einstein's 1916 manuscript on his general theory of relativity is handwritten.

astronomy professor and foreign correspondent for the Royal Astronomical Society (RAS) of London. De Sitter wrote three articles explaining the theory in monthly notices for the RAS, which were published by RAS Secretary Arthur Eddington. As relations were bad between scientists on opposing sides of the war, de Sitter and Eddington were the first to expose the non-German-speaking world to general relativity. Eddington, together with British astronomer Frank Dyson, decided to photograph a 1919 eclipse to test the theory.

In Berlin, Einstein was sought after, as people wanted to ask the young scientist questions about his remarkable ideas. In 1916, he wrote a book called *Relativity: The Special and the General Theory*, which explained his theories to readers who were curious but who were not specialists in the mathematics of theoretical physics.

So How Does the General Theory Work?

Like special relativity, general relativity is challenging to imagine because it is beyond daily life and ordinary experiences. Einstein added gravity to special relativity and ended up creating a whole new way of thinking about the universe. A common way to describe his concept of space is to use the metaphor of a rubber sheet. Picture a large rubber sheet held in the air, and stretched tight and flat. If you added something heavy to it, such as a big iron ball, the sheet would dip down around the ball. Then, if you added smaller balls to the sheet, they would roll toward the bigger ball because of the dip.

Gravity is not a force that pulls things down, but a way of twisting space.

The sun is like the big iron ball, changing the fabric (or rubber sheet) of space, and the planets are like the smaller balls,

In a demonstration of the way gravity curves space, children roll balls on an elastic sheet at Boston's Museum of Science, in 2004.

responding to the sun's curve (or dip) in space. The sun is not the only object with a heavy mass in space, so other bodies also change the curves or dips of the universe. In fact, all objects warp or dent the imaginary rubber sheet of space, but some have incredibly small effects. The more mass a body has, the greater the effect it has. Thus, the earth warps space, but less than Jupiter does, which warps it less than the sun. American physicist John Wheeler explained it this way: "Space tells matter how to move and matter tells space how to curve." All things, including light, follow the shortest path as they travel along the contours of space. Gravity is not a force that pulls things down, but a way of twisting space.

In the same way, a person standing on the earth has very little mass compared to the earth. Earth's effect in twisting space makes it feel like a person is being pulled down toward the surface of the earth.

In 1916, Karl Schwarzschild, a German astrophysicist who was fighting on the Russian front, studied the general theory of relativity. Like Einstein, Schwarzschild was able to focus on science regardless of the war that was going on around him. He was able to use general relativity to put together ideas about the existence of what would ultimately become known as "black holes." While in Russia, Schwarzschild wrote a paper about black holes and another using general relativity. Shortly thereafter, he became ill and was brought back to Berlin, where he died in May 1916. Einstein gave a memorial address for him.

Using Einstein's theory of general relativity, German astrophysicist Karl Schwarzschild came to formulate the theory behind "black holes."

Black Holes

Black holes are big stars that have collapsed in on themselves. They are so dense and massive, not even light can move fast enough to escape their gravitational field. Astrophysicists study black holes for clues about how the universe might have developed.

In 1939, when American physicists J. Robert Oppenheimer and Hartland Snyder were working with general relativity, they published a paper proposing that stars could collapse to become the large mass–small size objects Schwarzschild described.

It's hard to prove the existence of black holes. You can't see them directly because no light escapes from them. But scientists study the way other objects act around them to calculate their locations. Since scientists can't say positively whether they are indeed black holes, they're called "black hole candidates." The first black hole candidate to be found in space was Cygnus X-1, seven thousand light-years away from Earth, found in 1965. A dozen other strong candidates have been found since.

This is an artist's rendition of a spinning black hole. It was inspired by the theory that as black holes suck objects in, they may spin, pulling the fabric of the cosmos around them.

CHAPTER 9

Life with Einstein

What I admired most in him [Michele Besso] as a human being is that he managed to live for so many years not only in peace but also in lasting harmony with a woman.

Einstein's general theory of relativity was finally completed to his satisfaction, but the following year was not all smooth sailing. At Easter time in 1916, he went to visit Mileva, seeking a divorce. The visit went so badly that Mileva had a breakdown, and Einstein decided not to see her again, giving up on the idea of divorce for the moment. Hans Albert stopped writing his father, so Michele Besso kept Einstein informed about how his children and their mother were doing. Besso also became the divorce negotiator between Mileva and Einstein.

Einstein had suffered from stomach troubles off and on for years, but in 1917, they became much more serious. He was

After divorcing Mileva in 1919, Albert married his cousin Elsa Löwenthal a few months later. Elsa and Albert are shown together in this undated photograph.

reported to have had gallstones, liver and stomach problems, and ulcers. Wartime food didn't help, but at least he had a dedicated caregiver in Elsa. He was only thirty-eight years old, but a visitor to his sickbed asked him whether he was afraid of dying. Einstein replied to him, "I feel myself so much a part of all life that I am not in the least concerned with the beginning or end of the concrete existence of any particular person in this unending stream."

A Cosmological Constant

Although Einstein lost about fifty-six pounds during his illness and his recovery would take four years, he was able to be productive. In February 1917, he used the general theory of relativity to come up with a model of the universe. Relativity suggested that gravity would change the size of the universe, but because people at that time believed the universe was unchanging, he introduced a "cosmological constant" to explain how it could stay the same.

Five years later, Russian mathematician and meteorologist Alexander Friedmann, using the general relativity equations, concluded that the universe began as a hot and intensely dense core of energy that spread out and cooled over time. In 1927, Belgian astronomer (and Catholic priest) Georges Lemaître confirmed Friedmann's work and thought: If the universe is expanding

Russian scientist Alexander Friedmann, shown in a photo taken in Moscow, used Einstein's general relativity equations to help put forth his theory on how the universe began. Astronomer (and priest) Georges Lemaître then proposed the explosion of a primeval atom, which became known as "the big bang."

now, at some point it must have been closer together. What was it like when it was completely together? Lemaître proposed that the universe began with the explosion of an original atom (later known as "the big bang"). Two years later, American astronomer Edwin Hubble provided important concrete evidence about the expansion of the universe. He observed that galaxies were moving away from the earth in every direction.

Einstein decided to retract his cosmological constant, calling it his "biggest blunder." And for many years, it was considered to be a mistake. Ironically, in 1998, scientists began revisiting the possibility that he was right all along. His cosmological constant seems to match the behavior of "dark energy," a mysterious form of energy which explains why the universe has been expanding more quickly. Einstein would have been surprised to see his "blunder" given new life.

Scientists of Einstein's time questioned whether the universe remains static or if it changes. Those who believed the universe changes speculated how it might change by expanding or contracting. This chart compares various theories, showing how they relate to one another.

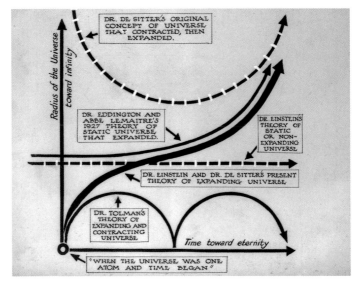

Edwin Hubble

Edwin Hubble was born in Missouri in 1889. After becoming a lawyer, he realized that what he really wanted to do was study astronomy. Hubble went back to school to get a PhD in astronomy and then, after a tour of duty in World War I, he went to work at the Mount Wilson Observatory in California.

At the observatory, Hubble studied galaxies outside our own Milky Way. In 1929, he conceived "Hubble's Law," which described the expansion of the universe and also helped astronomers date the age of the universe.

The Hubble Space Telescope, named in Edwin Hubble's honor, was launched by the space shuttle *Discovery* in 1990, thirty-seven years after Edwin Hubble's death. The Hubble Space Telescope has taken more than seven hundred thousand images of space in its first fifteen years and continues to circle the earth every ninety-seven minutes!

Through his observations of the galaxies, American astronomer Edwin Hubble provided proof that the universe was expanding. Hubble (center) is shown in this 1931 photograph with Albert Einstein looking into the 100-inch Hooker telescope at the Mount Wilson Observatory in California. Astronomer Walter Adams is to the right.

The Trouble with Albert

In October 1917, Einstein finally became the director of the Kaiser Wilhelm Institute for Physics. Due to the war, the "Institute" was just his apartment. Its (and his) primary task at that point was to furnish research grants to university scientists. Elsa's daughter, Ilse, became Einstein's secretary in January 1918.

Working closely with Ilse seemed to give Einstein ideas. That spring, he asked Ilse if she would consider marrying him—even though he was already engaged to her mother. Elsa said that she would be willing to step aside if it would make her daughter happy, but Ilse said no.

A 1920 portrait of Einstein in profile shows his some-what unruly hair.

Elsa's tolerance of Einstein's unusual behavior had been tested many times before, especially when it came to his appearance. Back in 1913, she gave him a hairbrush and tried to encourage him to take better care of himself. He was offended, however, and told her she'd better accept him as he was. Another time, when she prompted him to wear proper attire to the office, he said, "Why should I? Everybody

"God has put so much into him that is beautiful, and I find him wonderful, even though life at his side is debilitating and difficult in every respect."

Albert and Elsa Einstein, who became world travelers, are shown together in Egypt, c. 1928.

knows me there." On another occasion, when she suggested he dress properly for a conference, he replied, "Why should I? Nobody knows me there." She didn't quite give up, although she never made any progress.

It wasn't just his personal appearance that Elsa had to tolerate. Fidelity was not Einstein's strong suit, either. After Michele Besso's death (in 1955, only a month before his own), Einstein wrote to Michele's family: "What I admired most in him as a human being is that he managed to live for so many years not only in peace but also in lasting harmony with a woman—an undertaking in which I twice failed rather miserably." Elsa said about Einstein, "God has put so much into him that is beautiful, and I find him wonderful, even though life at his side is debilitating and difficult in every respect."

Einstein and Mileva's divorce came through on Valentine's Day, 1919. His adultery was used as the reason for the divorce, and in their settlement, he agreed to give Mileva any Nobel Prize money he won in the future. Einstein married Elsa in Berlin on June 2, 1919.

A Miraculous Eclipse of the Sun

During the war, German scientists were asked not to refer to British scientists in footnotes unless absolutely necessary. Cooperation between British and German scientists had been unthinkable. But now that World War I was over—having ended in November 1918—collaboration between the countries was possible. Arthur Eddington, the Royal Astronomical Society scientist who first learned about general relativity in 1915 through Willem de Sitter, prepared expeditions to Príncipe Island (a tiny island off the coast of western Africa in the Gulf of Guinea) and to Sobral, Brazil, to take photographs of the May 29, 1919, eclipse. If the sun's gravitational field caused the starlight to curve the way Einstein had predicted, his theory of relativity would be upheld.

Because the weather was an important and uncontrollable part of the experiment, two expeditions were sent to photograph the eclipse. As it turned out, the weather was uncooperative on Príncipe Island, but it was clear in Brazil. It is fortunate the Brazil

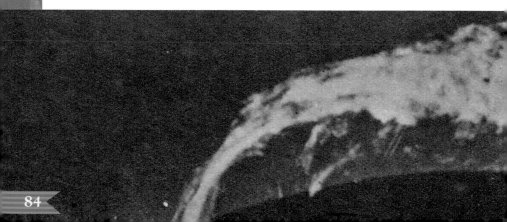

expedition used two telescopes to photograph the event.

Finding out whether the photographs confirmed Einstein's calculations took several months. In September, it was confirmed that the measurements from the expeditions' photos had verified Einstein's work, but it wasn't until November 6 that the conclusions were formally announced in London. Based on the teachings and theories of Isaac Newton (1642–1727), the calculations presented were not possible. The fact that Einstein's ideas were confirmed and Isaac Newton's long-standing ideas were refuted caused a scientific uproar. The next day, the *London Times* newspaper ran the headline: "Revolution in science —New theory of the Universe —Newtonian ideas overthrown."

Some physicists weren't convinced that the evidence was particularly strong, but the general public was impressed. (Stronger support would come from future eclipses and other tests.) Einstein's reputation among physicists had been growing since 1905, but now the rest of the world had heard about him, too. Not very many scientists ever become household names, but Albert Einstein would become an international celebrity almost overnight.

British observers in Brazil capture the famed solar eclipse of May 1919. Photographs confirmed Einstein's theory of relativity.

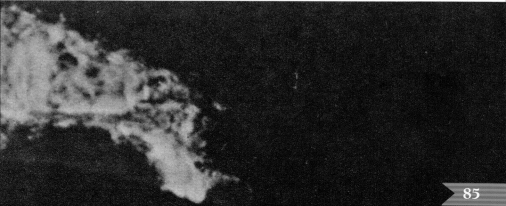

CHAPTER 10

World Citizen

One can be international minded without being indifferent to one's kinsmen.

Although Einstein was a person who enjoyed privacy, he accepted his celebrity with surprisingly good humor. His political passions motivated him to speak out on issues. Einstein's interest in international politics had been growing since the start of World War I. After the end of the war, he reevaluated his feelings about Germany.

Instead of having a kaiser (emperor), the country had become a republic. Einstein was excited about this change. In 1919, Germany was struggling with the aftermath of the war: lack of food; illness; a weakened economy; and anger about the severe penalties against Germany outlined in the Treaty of Versailles—the

Poverty in Germany after World War I, propelled by large-scale unemployment and high inflation, contributed to Adolf Hitler's rise in 1933.

This photograph, taken around 1930, shows Albert and Elsa Einstein at home in Germany.

agreement signed by the Germans and Allies to end World War I. Einstein was disappointed with the Allies for their harsh treatment of Germany.

That year, friends introduced Einstein to the concept of Zionism, which was a movement that supported a homeland for the Jewish people in Israel. Even though he was not an observant Jew, he liked the idea. He did not feel that his interests in Zionism and internationalism contradicted each other, saying, "One can be international minded without being indifferent to one's kinsmen." He might not have followed Jewish law, but he felt he had a kinship with his fellow Jews.

Einstein wrote, "So long as I lived in Switzerland, I did not become aware of my Jewishness. . . . This changed as soon as I took up residency in Berlin." In Germany, Einstein saw anti-Semitism (prejudice against Jewish people) hinder Jews in their studies and in their jobs. He would experience anti-Semitism firsthand in 1920, when he saw the reactions to his theory of relativity.

On February 20, 1920, Einstein's mother, Pauline, died. She had come to live with Einstein and Elsa at the end of December, already very ill with cancer. "One feels in one's bones the significance of blood ties," he wrote a friend, speaking about Pauline's death.

Defending Relativity

In his professional life, Einstein's theory of relativity was not accepted without question, although people were fascinated with the idea. Einstein found that scientists who resisted new ideas were suspicious of it, and people who disliked Einstein for being Jewish or for his international beliefs renounced the new theory. "The world is a curious madhouse," Einstein wrote. He had noticed that everyone—not just scientists, but the average person as well—had an opinion about whether relativity was correct. But most of their opinions, he observed, were based on politics rather than on an understanding of the science.

Some of the "non-believers" took extraordinary steps to disparage Einstein's theory. An unknown named Paul Weyland created an "Association of Natural German Scientists for the Preservation of Pure Science" that was dedicated to opposing relativity. He held an anti-Semitic public meeting on August 24, 1920, and spoke out against relativity. Einstein himself came to see what they said and he wrote an angry letter to a newspaper about it, which was printed three days later.

At the meeting, Weyland verbally attacked Einstein and mentioned physicist Philipp Lenard's name in his speech. Lenard already knew Einstein and had issues with Einstein's theory. Although Weyland had used Lenard's name without permission, Einstein was not aware of this, and he included harsh words for Lenard in his letter to the newspaper. This, in turn angered

Lenard, and a debate between the two was arranged for September 23.

At their debate, Lenard contended that relativity went against common sense, and he threw in a few anti-Semitic remarks with his comments. Einstein defended himself. But Lenard and Einstein would never be on good terms again. Paul Weyland went back into obscurity, and the anti-relativists failed.

Becoming an International Celebrity

Leaving Germany for a less anti-Semitic location crossed Einstein's mind at this time, but he would continue to stay until things took a distinct turn for the worse. He made his first trip to the United States in April 1921. While there, he was welcomed to the White House by President Warren G. Harding.

During his visit to the United States, Einstein gave lectures to

On his first trip to the United States, Albert Einstein met President Warren Harding (shown here, center) in April 1921.

raise money for the proposed Hebrew University in Jerusalem. Einstein saw that Jewish students weren't allowed to attend universities in Germany and he thought the Hebrew University would be a good idea. During that entire decade he would also offer free courses on relativity to Jewish and Eastern European students who were shut out of his classes in Berlin.

His 1921 visit also included receiving an honorary degree from Princeton University, where Einstein would later come to work after fleeing Germany. One of his statements during this Princeton stay would become famous: "Subtle is the Lord, but malicious he is not." By that, he meant that nature was mysterious, but rational. Things made sense, even if they were complex and hard to figure out.

In an ironic turn of events, Einstein won the 1921 Nobel Prize in Physics for his 1905 photoelectricity paper (about light particles), not for his relativity theories.

This feeling of Einstein's—that nature should make sense—would spur him to argue against quantum physics for the rest of his life, even though he had jump-started quantum theories with his own proposal that light was both a particle and a wave.

In an ironic turn of events, Einstein won the 1921 Nobel Prize in Physics for his 1905 photoelectricity paper (about light particles), not for his relativity theories. The announcement that he had won the Nobel Prize was made in November 1922, when Einstein was on his way to Japan to lecture and sightsee.

A truly interested "citizen of the world," Albert Einstein visited and lectured in Prague, Austria, France, Japan, Singapore, Hong Kong, and Palestine between 1922 and 1923. He kept diaries as he traveled the world, chronicling what he had learned about other cultures. Being a celebrity suited him, if not his stomach condition.

In 1922, Einstein received an interesting paper from an unknown Indian physicist named Satyendra Nath Bose. Bose had been working on statistics about how large numbers of photons would behave. This project sparked Einstein's curiosity, inspiring him to add ideas of his own. In 1925, they published the Bose-Einstein paper on condensation, the process by which a gas or vapor changes to a liquid.

Friends and Relations

Around 1921 Einstein met Danish physicist Niels Bohr. Bohr and Einstein had famous debates on whether it was possible to precisely measure a particle at a particular moment.

Since he felt as though everything should be able to be predicted, Einstein insisted that it could be done, and he came up with experiments intending to prove it. Bohr, however, would always find a reason why the experiments wouldn't work. Although his colleague won the debates, Einstein never gave up. A physicist version of the "Why did the chicken cross the road?" joke is: "Why did Einstein cross the road?" The answer is, "To get away from Niels Bohr, only he found that Bohr was there, too."

At the October 1927 Solvay Conference, Niels Bohr and Einstein had a famous exchange of words. Einstein was not happy

Niels Bohr consistently challenged Einstein's ideas. He won the Nobel Prize for Physics in 1922, just one year after Einstein won the same prize.

The Bose-Einstein Condensation Theory

The Bose-Einstein condensation theory predicts that atoms, if cooled to nearly absolute zero (around −460 degrees Fahrenheit, or −273 degrees Celsius), have such low energy that they act as one giant "mono-atom." This idea seemed ridiculous in 1925 and was impossible to prove because of the limits of technology at the time. It wasn't until 1995 that the first Bose-Einstein condensate was created in a laboratory. Today, physicists study these condensates with great interest. American scientists Eric Cornell and Carl Wiemann won the 2001 Nobel Prize in Physics for creating Bose-Einstein condensates.

Einstein collaborated with physicist Satyendra Nath Bose, of India (shown here in 1925), to produce the Bose-Einstein paper on condensation.

with the unpredictability of quantum mechanics and he complained, "God does not play dice with the universe." To this, Niels Bohr answered that Einstein should stop telling God what to do.

In addition to his physics work, Einstein felt that scholars, including scientists, had a duty to work for the public good. He did his best to live up to that ideal. In 1925, he joined Indian leader Mahatma Gandhi in signing a manifesto against compulsory military service. Gandhi's ability to lead a nonviolent revolution impressed Einstein, who admired him all his life. "Gandhi, the greatest political genius of our time, indicated the path to be taken," Einstein wrote.

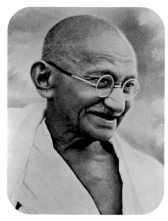

A 1940s photograph of the Indian leader Mohandas "Mahatma" Gandhi, who was joined by Einstein in a fight against forced military service.

On the personal side, Einstein's stepdaughter Ilse married journalist Rudolf Kayser in 1924. Rudolf would one day write a biography about his father-in-law. In 1927, Hans Albert married Frieda Knecht, against his father's wishes. Einstein had found his own parents' disapproval aggravating when he wanted to marry Mileva, but he couldn't keep himself from expressing his own displeasure with Hans Albert's choice. However, Hans Albert would prove to be happier in his marriage to Frieda than Einstein was with Mileva.

Travel, work, and celebrity finally took its toll on Einstein, and in 1928 he developed a heart condition that would force him to stay in bed. In April, Helen Dukas began working for him as his secretary. She would prove to be an important person in Einstein's life, staying with him as both his secretary and his housekeeper (after Elsa died).

The Einsteins had a summer house built in Caputh, Germany, and when Einstein turned fifty in 1929, he was back on his feet and able to appreciate his birthday gift: a sailboat. In addition to music making and pipe smoking, sailing was his chief hobby.

The year 1930 brought both joy and tragedy to Einstein's family. Hans Albert and his wife made Einstein a grandfather with the birth of their son Bernhard Caesar Einstein. But to the family's sorrow, Einstein's second son, Eduard (Tete) began

Niels Bohr

Danish scientist Niels Bohr was born in 1885. He was very close to his younger brother, Harald, who won a silver medal on to Danish Olympic soccer team in 1908. Niels won the 1922 Nobel Prize in Physics for his research into the structure of atoms and their radiation. He was a well-respected theoretical physicist, which is why he was such a good, if frustrating, debating companion for Einstein in the 1920s and 1930s.

In 1943, during Denmark's occupation by the Nazis, Bohr, who was of Jewish ancestry, became aware that the German police were going to arrest him. He escaped to Sweden, then ended up in New Mexico, working on the Manhattan Project, which was the United States' effort to make an atom bomb.

Danish scientist Niels Bohr and Einstein met and had a lively exchange. This photograph of the two of them relaxing together was taken by physicist and mathematician Paul Ehrenfest.

After the war, Niels returned to Copenhagen and died there in 1951. He is pictured on Danish money, the 500 kronen bill.

showing signs of schizophrenia. His condition would worsen over the decade, causing this once excellent student to give up his studies. Mileva would spend the rest of her life tending to Tete. Einstein would visit them for the last time in 1933.

During the latter half of 1930, Einstein traveled again to the United States. He made a point of visiting Edwin Hubble, at the California Institute of Technology (Caltech), and was so convinced by Hubble's evidence of an expanding universe that he threw out his cosmological constant altogether. While he was in the United States, Einstein visited many other American friends. Einstein's celebrity status brought him in touch with other well-known people, such as Upton Sinclair, author of *The Jungle*, a novel exposing the horrors of Chicago's meatpacking industry. Einstein appreciated Sinclair's efforts on behalf of workers, and they met each other in 1930.

On that same visit, Einstein also went with famous actor Charlie Chaplin to the opening of Chaplin's movie *City Lights* in January 1931. Chaplin is said to have told Einstein, "They cheer me because they all understand me, and they cheer you because no one understands you."

Never one to take himself too seriously, Einstein viewed his

During their 1931 tour of the United States, Albert and Elsa Einstein visited the Hopi House at the Grand Canyon in Arizona.

Albert became friendly with many American celebrities while visiting the United States. He is shown here in February 1931 with actor Charlie Chaplin at the premiere of Chaplin's *City Lights*.

own fame with an amused eye. "To punish me for my contempt for authority, Fate has made me an authority myself," he commented in 1930.

Shortly after his U.S. trip, Caltech asked Einstein to come and work there, but Princeton won out. In August 1932, he accepted an appointment to the Institute for Advanced Study at Princeton. His intentions were to spend half of each year in the United States and half in Germany, but by the end of 1932, it was clear that the Nazis would make that impossible. "Take a good look at it, you will never see it again," he told Elsa of their Caputh home. He would prove right: Once they left Germany on December 10, 1932, they would never return.

Although the Einsteins' house in Caputh, Germany, was a peaceful and enjoyable place to live, once they left in December 1932, they never returned.

CHAPTER 11

Before and After World War II

Had I known that the Germans would not succeed in producing an atomic bomb, I never would have lifted a finger.

The **Fascist** National Socialist German Workers (Nazi) Party, led by Adolf Hitler, took power in Germany on January 30, 1933. That year, Nazis searched Einstein's old home, confiscated his belongings, and burned books that he had written. His photograph was posted in the official "Enemies of the State" book, with the caption reading, "Not yet hanged."

In October, Einstein gave a speech in London at a fund-raiser to help academics who were fleeing Germany. He had realized that **pacifism** would not work in every situation, and urged Western Europeans to prepare themselves to oppose the Nazi regime. His pacifist friends were startled by his change of heart, but Einstein still wanted to work for peace. He just didn't think the Nazis could be fought with peaceful methods.

Einstein spent the months between December 1932 and October 1933 traveling to various places (first in the United States and then in Europe). In October, Albert Einstein arrived as a refugee in Princeton, New Jersey, with his wife, Elsa; secretary, Helen Dukas; and assistant, Walther Mayer, who was an Austrian-Jewish mathematician.

Helen Dukas, Einstein's secretary, immigrated to the United States with Albert and his wife. She is shown here taking dictation from Einstein in Le Coq-sur-Mer, Belgium, in 1933.

When Einstein arrived in the United States, he did not know how to speak English. German had been the official "language of science," so there had been no need for him to learn English while he was working in Europe. Einstein was now fifty-four years old—not an age at which a person usually learns a new language, but he did a good job learning it. Still, when he was

Einstein specifically requested that his home in Princeton, New Jersey, not be made into a memorial.

asked to give a lecture or write a letter or paper in English, he would write it in German and have someone translate it.

Although he was safe now, Einstein did not forget the Jews left behind in Germany. Not only were his own relatives begging him for help, strangers also sent him pleading letters. Einstein wrote affidavits (legal written statements) on behalf of so many people that by the end of the 1930s, he feared that his name on an affidavit had lost its influence.

Elsa's daughter Margot joined them in Princeton in 1934, but her other daughter, Ilse, died in Paris that same year after a long illness. In August 1935, Einstein and Elsa bought a house at 112 Mercer Street, their final home. He specifically requested that the house not be turned into a memorial, so it is still a private residence today.

Scientific Work in Princeton

In 1935, Einstein—together with Russian physicist Boris Podolsky and Israeli physicist Nathan Rosen—introduced the Einstein-Podolsky-Rosen (EPR) **paradox**. The paradox was intended by the three colleagues to point out where quantum mechanics fails. However, the EPR paradox did not end up discrediting quantum mechanics. It indicated that unexplained things happened and that quantum mechanics violated long-held expectations—something that Einstein knew and disliked all along. In any event, the paradox ended up being helpful to physicists because it started them thinking along new lines. Einstein was very good at that, even when it wasn't his intention.

The following year, Einstein presented another concept that contemporary scientists continue to put in service: microlensing. Microlensing is when one star's gravitational field acts as a magnifier for another, more distant star. He admitted that this

Although he wasn't coming up with earthshaking ideas like relativity, Einstein's ideas kept sending scientists off in new directions.

would be a rare occurrence and that he didn't think that there would be any way to see it happen directly.

Einstein would be pleasantly surprised to know that astronomers can see "Einstein rings" and "Einstein crosses" (named for Albert Einstein, naturally) with the microlensing effect. In January 2006, scientists announced they'd discovered the most "Earthlike planet yet"—called OGLE-2005-BLG-390Lb—by using the technique. Although he wasn't coming up with earthshaking ideas like relativity, Einstein's ideas kept sending scientists off in new directions.

In 1936, Einstein's son Hans Albert received his doctorate from Einstein's old school, the ETH, in Switzerland. In December the same year, Elsa died after a long illness. Her marriage to Einstein was fairly functional but not close, and her passing did not affect him very much. With Elsa gone, Helen Dukas and Margot tended to his personal needs. In 1939, Einstein's sister, Maja, joined the household, when she fled Fascist Italy.

Fighting Discrimination

Princeton provided a safe location for Einstein—away from Germany—but it was not without its racial injustices. At that time, the university limited the number of Jewish students it would accept, and there were only two Jewish faculty members. African-Americans couldn't attend at all. Einstein became aware of these discriminations and set about to battle not only anti-Semitism, but all **racism**.

When W. E. B. DuBois, the head of the National Association for the Advancement of Colored People (NAACP), asked him to say a few words for their magazine, Einstein sent back a reply that

Albert Einstein took every opportunity to stand up for what he thought was right.

spoke warmly about supporting the "determined effort of American Negroes" to oppose race prejudice. And when he heard about the "Scottsboro Boys" incident involving nine African-American teenagers falsely accused of raping two white women, he joined the campaign to save them.

Albert Einstein took every opportunity to stand up for what he thought was right. In 1937, he stepped in when African-American opera star Marian Anderson was refused a room at Princeton's Nassau Inn. He invited her to stay at his home, which she did. From then on, she stayed with him whenever she visited Princeton. Einstein would also make friends with another prominent African-American singer—Paul Robeson—but that friendship would later bring him to the attention of the FBI (Federal Bureau of Investigation).

The Atom Bomb

At the end of 1938, Europe was the site of a momentous discovery: the first successful fission experiments, part of the Manhattan Project. Scientists such as Italian Enrico Fermi had been working on the idea for several years, but it wasn't until Otto Hahn, Lise Meitner, Fritz Strassmann, and Otto Frisch put the pieces together that nuclear fission seemed viable. Word spread quickly, and Hungarian physicist Leo Szilard realized that Germany might try to make a bomb with this new knowledge. He approached Einstein about it in July 1939.

Marian Anderson

Philadelphia native Marian Anderson did not have her first voice lesson until she was fifteen years old, in 1912. She was turned away from the music school of her choice because she was African-American. As a prize for winning a singing contest, she debuted in 1925 with the New York Philharmonic Orchestra. Afterward, she received a fellowship, which enabled her to travel through Europe, where there was less racial prejudice.

As her career took off, critics and music-lovers around the world praised her. Composer Jean Sibelius dedicated his work *Solitude* to Anderson. Italian conductor Arturo Toscanini declared, "A voice like yours is only heard once in a hundred years."

In 1939, the Daughters of the American Revolution (DAR) refused to let Marian Anderson sing at Constitution Hall in Washington, D.C., because of her race. Anderson sang instead on the steps of the Lincoln Memorial to a live audience of seventy-five thousand. This event is one of the most famous concerts in American history.

In 1939, Marian Anderson sang on the steps of the Lincoln Memorial when the DAR refused to let her sing at Constitution Hall.

This 1946 photograph of Albert Einstein and Leo Szilard shows the two physicists reenacting the signing of their 1939 letter to President Roosevelt, which informed the president of the Nazi's intention to build an atom bomb.

Szilard, together with physicist Eugene Wigner, discussed with Einstein the possibility of the Nazis building an atomic bomb. Uranium—a metallic radioactive element—was a key ingredient, so they hoped to keep Belgium's significant uranium supplies out of Hitler's hands by having Einstein contact his friend, the Belgian queen. He agreed, but then unofficial presidential adviser Alexander Sachs suggested that Einstein write U.S. President Franklin Delano Roosevelt about the atom bomb problem instead.

Together, Szilard and Einstein wrote the letter and dated it August 2, 1939, but it wasn't until October 11 that Roosevelt received word of the letter—more than a month after Germany had invaded Poland and World War II had begun. President

The Manhattan Project

The Manhattan Project was the name of the project to create the atom bomb in the United States during World War II. The name comes from the location of Columbia University in New York City, where early research for the project was carried out.

The earliest research for making a bomb was really conducted by scientists who discovered fission. Fission is the splitting of a nucleus into at least two smaller nuclei. It causes the release of a relatively large amount of energy. Fission occurs when an atom's nucleus is bombarded by neutrons, or it can occur naturally. It can be described as "the splitting of atoms." Once scientists figured out how to control fission, an atomic bomb became possible. The first self-sustaining nuclear chain reaction took place in a laboratory built under the bleachers of the football field at the University of Chicago.

The project began in 1942, and the following year, a laboratory was created at Los Alamos, New Mexico, dedicated to the making of the bomb. Physicist J. Robert Oppenheimer was the head of the scientific portion of the project, and General Leslie R. Groves was in charge of the administrative side.

A test bomb was exploded near Alamogordo, New Mexico, on July 16, 1945, three weeks before the bomb was dropped on Hiroshima, Japan.

Enrico Fermi (seated, looking at papers) is shown at Los Alamos during the Manhattan Project. Head of the project was J. Robert Oppenheimer, seated to the right of Fermi.

On October 1, 1940, Albert Einstein officially became a U.S. citizen. He is shown here taking the oath of U.S. citizenship along with Helen Dukas (left) and his daughter Margot Einstein (right).

Roosevelt appointed an advisory committee on uranium, but it wasn't until August 1942 that the Manhattan Project was established to create the first nuclear weapon. Despite the warning letter he had sent to the president, Einstein was not allowed to work on the Manhattan Project because he was considered too much of a security risk. However, he was invited to work for the U.S. Navy as a high-explosives adviser in 1943.

Einstein received his U.S. citizenship in 1940. He'd been asked if he wanted to get his citizenship earlier through an act of Congress, but Einstein wanted to become an American citizen the same way everyone else did. He kept his Swiss nationality as well, so he remained a dual citizen for the rest of his life. To raise money for the war effort, Einstein wrote out his original special relativity paper by hand in 1944, which sold for $6 million at auction. The manuscript is now housed in the Library of Congress.

In March 1945, Einstein wrote President Roosevelt again, asking him to let Leo Szilard express his concerns about dropping an atom bomb. The scientists involved in this project had not realized that they would not have a say as to how their work would be used. Unfortunately, the president died of a cerebral hemorrhage on April 12 and most likely never saw Einstein's letter. In July, scientists who worked on the Manhattan Project wrote petitions against dropping the bomb on Japan

Hiroshima and Nagasaki

The destruction caused by the bombs that fell on Hiroshima and Nagasaki was devastating. Out of the 255,000 people living in Hiroshima at that time, 66,000 were killed and 69,000 were injured, for a total of 135,00 casualties. Nagasaki had a population of 195,000; 39,000 were killed, and 25,000 were wounded by the bomb (64,000 total). The emotional pain of the survivors is something that can't be added to the calculation.

The damage to the cities themselves was intense. The moment of explosion caused a radiation of heat and light that caused "flash burns" on people and also started fires. Those fires spread to create a "firestorm" in Hiroshima (but not in Nagasaki, because of the geography of the city). In both locations, everything within a mile from the center of the explosion was destroyed. Everything within three miles was heavily damaged.

This August 1945 photograph shows the devastation of Hiroshima, Japan, after being hit by an atomic bomb.

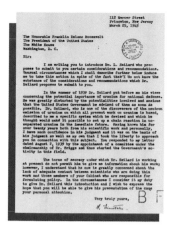

In this letter to President Franklin Delano Roosevelt in March of 1945, Albert Einstein expressed his concerns about the atom bomb.

without a warning. The first bomb fell on Hiroshima, Japan, on August 6, 1945. Three days later, a second bomb was dropped on Nagasaki, Japan.

As a humanitarian, the loss of life came as a blow to Einstein. And when the Smyth Report, by physicist Henry DeWolf Smyth, was released in August, it became general knowledge that it was Einstein who had encouraged the making of the bomb in his 1939 letter to the president. Einstein's image was tinged with tragic overtones as his name was linked with the atomic bomb. Einstein later commented, "Had I known that the Germans would not succeed in producing an atomic bomb, I never would have lifted a finger."

World War II affected Einstein in other ways as well. He lost relatives in concentration camps and he feared greatly for Jews and others who had been subject to the Third Reich. Albert Einstein's modified stance on pacifism disgruntled his previous allies, and his social concerns angered some politicians in his new country.

The cover of *Time* magazine on July 1, 1946, featured Albert Einstein with a mushroom cloud from an atomic explosion in the background. The headline read, "Cosmoclast Einstein: All matter is speed and flame."

CHAPTER 12

The Final Years

There is no greater satisfaction for a just and well-meaning person than the knowledge that he has devoted his best energies to the services of the good cause.

In 1945, Einstein officially retired from Princeton's Institute for Advanced Study, but he still held an office there until his death. His work—which largely consisted of trying to create a "unified field theory" that would combine quantum physics and relativity—would remain important to him until the end.

On December 10, 1945, Einstein gave a speech at a Nobel Prize dinner entitled "The war is won, but the peace is not." He was so passionate about making the world a more peaceful place that he and Leo Szilard founded the Emergency Committee of Atomic Scientists (ECAS) the following year. The ECAS dedicated itself to educating the public about the dangers of nuclear weapons, as well as the advancement of world peace and benign uses of atomic energy. He also encouraged the United Nations to form a world government, believing that it was the key to peace.

A 2002 photograph of the United Nations Secretariat building at UN Headquarters in New York City.

Albert Einstein is shown sailing with his friend Johanna Fantova on Lake Carnegie in Princeton, New Jersey.

Although Einstein maintained his involvement in politics and science, he and his loved ones were becoming elderly. He turned sixty-seven in 1946, the same year his younger sister suffered a stroke and became bedridden. He would read to her every evening. Johanna Fantova, an old European friend who had moved to the United States in 1939, had become a fixture in his home. She was Einstein's last love interest, even though he hadn't been concerned about his appearance for a while. He explained, "It would be a sad situation if the wrapper were better than the meat wrapped inside it."

Continuing the Fight Against Racism

Racism in America was on Einstein's mind in his sixty-seventh year. Prompted by police crimes against African-Americans, in March 1946, he joined Eleanor Roosevelt's

National Committee for Justice, in Columbia, Tennessee. Although Einstein routinely turned down honorary degrees and requests to speak at universities, in May he came to the traditionally black Lincoln University in Pennsylvania. There, he received an honorary degree, spoke about racism, and then gave a lecture on relativity. The media, which generally covered his every move, skipped the event.

"I do not believe there is a way in which this deeply entrenched evil can be quickly healed," Einstein told the Lincoln University students. "But until this goal is reached, there is no greater satisfaction for a just and well-meaning person than the knowledge that he has devoted his best energies to the services of the good cause." Along these same lines that autumn, he would also tell the National Urban League (NUL) convention, "The worst disease from which the society of our nation suffers is . . . the treatment of the Negro."

The National Urban League

The movement of African-Americans from rural areas into New York City seeking better jobs and more freedom spurred the beginnings of the National Urban League in 1910. When the new-comers arrived in New York City, they found that they needed help, and Ruth Standish Baldwin and Dr. George Edmund Haynes founded the League in order to provide that support. By 1918, the organization had eighty-one staff members in thirty cities.

In 1963, the League hosted Martin Luther King, Jr., A. Philip Randolph, and other civil rights leaders in their planning meetings for the famous March on Washington, D.C. Today, the National Urban League has one hundred chapters in thirty-five states and Washington, D.C.

When singer Paul Robeson sent Einstein a telegram in September proposing the creation of "the American Crusade to End Lynching" (ACEL), Einstein supported him. Due to his ongoing stomach problems, Einstein wasn't well enough to come down for the ACEL rally in Washington—which was timed to correspond with the anniversary of the Emancipation Proclamation—but he did send a letter to President Harry Truman, asking him to draft an anti-lynching law. The ACEL bill was turned down, but in the process, the FBI submitted a twelve-page report on Einstein because of his association with Robeson, who was a known **Communist**.

In 1952, Paul Robeson and his friend, the writer Lloyd Brown, visited Einstein at his home. Lloyd tried to make small talk with Einstein when Paul had left the room, saying, "Dr. Einstein, it's really an honor to be in the presence of a great man." Einstein protested, "But you came in with a great man."

Taken on September 21, 1947, in Princeton, New Jersey, this photograph shows Einstein with his friend Paul Robeson (on the far right) as well as former vice president Henry Wallace (far left) and Princeton University's Lewis L. Wallace (third from the left).

McCarthyism

During the 1950s, Senator Joseph McCarthy conducted an extremist campaign to publicly expose well-known Americans he thought were Communists or Communist sympathizers. J. Edgar Hoover, director of the FBI, aided him. The climate in the United States during what became known as the McCarthy era worried Einstein because he felt the investigations to find Communists were more of a threat to democracy than the Communists were. He said that if he were choosing a profession in America at that time, he would have been a plumber or peddler rather than a scientist or scholar because he would have had more freedom.

As part of the House Un-American Activities Committee (HUAC), U.S. Representative John Rankin said, "It's about time the American people got wise to Einstein. . . . He ought to be prosecuted." Representative Rankin was also openly anti-Semitic. Einstein still spoke out openly against the authority of J. Edgar Hoover and Joseph McCarthy. He recommended that no one should testify before HUAC—where people were expected to "name names" of colleagues who might have Communist sympathies. Exercise civil disobedience, no matter what it costs you, he recommended.

Senator Joseph McCarthy would use fanatical measures to expose Americans he thought were Communists and Communist sympathizers. He is shown here (seated in the middle) at a June 7, 1954, hearing.

Perhaps McCarthy did not want to risk public disapproval by attacking an elderly legend, because he never charged Einstein as a Communist no matter how big Einstein's FBI file grew.

Active to the Very End

Mileva had died in 1948 after having a stroke, and Einstein, always struggling with stomach problems, had an abdominal operation that same year. He had an aneurysm (abnormal widening) of the major abdominal aorta, foreshadowing the cause of his death seven years later. He made out his will in 1950, leaving his violin to his grandson Bernhard and his papers to Hebrew University in Jerusalem.

Einstein's consistent support of Hebrew University and Jewish causes had not gone unnoticed. Israel had been formed in 1948, and when its president, Chaim Weizmann, died in 1952, Einstein was offered the presidency. He couldn't accept, but felt embarrassed when he turned it down.

For their part, Israel was perhaps relieved that this obstinately independent-minded man refused the job. David Ben-Gurion, the first prime minister of Israel, is reported to have said, "If he accepts, we are in for trouble."

That same year, a radioactive metal was discovered in

Albert Einstein loved to play his violin and is shown holding it in this image, c. 1930. In his will, written in 1950, he left his violin to his grandson Bernhard.

the debris from the first thermonuclear device explosion. The metal was designated a new chemical element and officially named "Einsteinium" for Albert Einstein in 1955. The atomic number for Einsteinium is 99.

Einstein's status as a world figure meant that people were constantly writing him with requests for autographs, quotes, advice—even for his shoes! For the most part, he was very generous with these inquiries. Even in the middle of the war, Einstein had still found time to correspond with his fans. To a junior high school student, he wrote reassuringly, in 1943, "Do not worry about your difficulties in mathematics; I can assure you that mine are still greater."

Revealing his ever-playful side, the famous photograph of

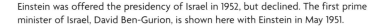

Einstein was offered the presidency of Israel in 1952, but declined. The first prime minister of Israel, David Ben-Gurion, is shown here with Einstein in May 1951.

Photographers asked Einstein to smile for a 72nd birthday portrait, and playful Albert stuck out his tongue instead.

Einstein sticking out his tongue was taken on his seventy-second birthday. He sent his doctor, Rudolf Nissen, a newspaper copy of the photo with the inscription: "To Nissen my tummy, the world my tongue!" In 1954, when he turned seventy-five, he received a favorite birthday card from old friends, who addressed their greetings to the "President of the Olympia Academy," the name

Einstein and his friends had called their discussion group back in Zurich.

His beloved friend Michele Besso died on March 15, 1955. Einstein wrote to Michele's family, "Now he has departed from this strange world a little ahead of me. That signifies nothing. For us believing physicists, the distinction between past, present, and future is only a stubbornly persistent illusion."

Signing the "[Bertrand] Russell-Einstein Manifesto," on April 11, 1955, was Albert Einstein's last public act. The manifesto warned of the horrible results of nuclear war and the importance of preventing one. Two days later, Einstein's abdominal aneurysm ruptured and he was admitted to Princeton Hospital. He asked that no extraordinary measures be taken to keep him alive. Even in his hospital room, Albert Einstein worked on his physics equations. He never gave up hope that he could solve the puzzle that had stumped him for so long. His last words were in German to a nurse who didn't understand them, and he died on April 18, 1955, at 1:15 a.m.

His Legacy

After Albert Einstein's death, the general public continued to be fascinated with his work and his life. He wasn't eager to have people trekking to "worship his bones," so he requested that his body be cremated and the ashes be scattered privately. Thomas Harvey, the hospital pathologist who saw Einstein after his death, preserved the physicist's brain before the cremation and kept it at his home. Decades would pass before scientists would study Albert Einstein's brain. He had said that he had not minded his brain being studied, but he

Even in his hospital room, Albert Einstein worked on his physics equations.

didn't want the results publicized. His wishes would not be followed in that regard.

Today, Albert Einstein's theories are being used all over the world in both practical, everyday things and in scientists' laboratories, where they are evaluating cosmic truths.

Scientists continue to study relativity to see if it holds up under every circumstance.

His theory of relativity passed yet another test with the discovery of binary pulsars. Russell Hulse and Joseph Taylor were awarded the 1993 Nobel Prize in Physics for discovering a binary pulsar back in 1974. A pulsar is like a cosmic lighthouse—a neutron star that emits pulses of energy. The binary pulsar that became known as the

Enjoying life, this 1933 photograph of Einstein on a bike was taken in Santa Barbara, California, at his friends' home.

Hulse-Taylor binary pulsar was watched for almost twenty years, and the behavior they found matched Einstein's theory of relativity. Scientists are still searching for the "unified theory" that eluded Einstein.

Still in the Public's Eye

In 1978, artist Robert Berks sculpted a bronze statue of Albert Einstein that stands outside of the National Academy of Sciences (NAS), in Washington, D.C. Berks hoped to show how the physicist was able to "travel the universe" with just a pad of paper and a pen. His statue depicts Albert Einstein holding a sheet of paper with three of his most famous equations: $E = mc^2$, one for general relativity, and one for the photoelectric effect.

In December 1999, *Time* magazine named Albert Einstein its "Person of the Century."

The year 2005 was a special one for Albert Einstein fans because the United Nations named it the "World Year of Physics" in honor of the hundred-year anniversary of his "Miracle Year." Celebrations ranged from plays, lectures, and books to a worldwide relay of lights called "the Light of Einstein." Canada's Perimeter Institute for Theoretical Physics held a month-long "EinsteinFest," which even included dozens of people dressed as Albert Einstein.

In December 1999, Time magazine named Albert Einstein its "Person of the Century."

Einstein's image is so meaningful to the public even today that Hebrew University in Jerusalem, which holds the copyright to all his personal papers, earns about a million dollars a year in royalties. In addition to pictures of his ever-popular wild mane and thoughtful face, you can spot his words on posters, T-shirts, mugs, and bookmarks, to name a few. People find inspiration in his science, his politics, and his sense of humor.

It's a rare human being who can turn the world upside down, but Albert Einstein did just that —with his creativity, belief in the beauty of science, and dogged determination.

"Imagination is more important than knowledge. Knowledge is limited. Imagination encircles the world."
—Albert Einstein

Located at the National Academy of Sciences in Washington, D.C., the Albert Einstein Memorial Statue by Robert Berks was unveiled in 1979.

Glossary

anti-Semitic—discriminating against Jewish people.

atomic clocks—extremely accurate clocks that are based on the vibrations of an atom or molecule.

Communist—a person who believes in a social system in which all property and means of production are owned in common and controlled by the state.

dissertation—a document written in completion of requirements for a doctorate degree at a university.

eclipse—the total or partial obscuring of one celestial body by another.

electrons—subatomic particles carrying a negative charge.

elliptical—having the form of an ellipse, or oval.

Fascist—part of a dictatorial government that forcibly controls its people, often by controlling businesses, suppressing opposition, and advocating extreme nationalism.

gravitational field—the area affected by the gravity associated with a body such as a planet or star.

industrial revolution—shift in the eighteenth and nineteenth century from an economy based on manual labor to one based on manufacturing.

kinetic—relating to motion or movement.

macroscopic—refers to objects large enough to be visible without the aid of a microscope.

mechanical engineering—the branch of engineering that deals with the design, construction and operation of machinery.

microscopic—refers to objects of extremely small size, visible only with the aid of a microscope.

Mosaic—of the teachings and principles of the prophet Moses.

MRI (magnetic resonance imaging) —a method to obtain images of the inside of different objects by influencing the magnetic fields of the object's atoms, especially used in medicine.

nuclear particle accelerator—a machine that boosts particles to nearly light speed and slams them together in order to probe the structure of matter.

Olympia—a Greek city where Mount Olympus is located, believed by ancient Greeks to be the dwelling place of the gods.

orbits—the paths of planets, stars, or other bodies around one another.

pacifism—opposition to the practice of war or violence.

paradox—a statement that appears to contradict itself.

patents—government documents granting a person sole rights to an invention for a certain number of years.

photoelectricity—electricity generated by light or affected by light.

quantum physics—the study of atomic and subatomic particles and the forces through which they interact.

racism—discrimination stemming from the belief that one "racial group" is inferior to another.

reference—a formal recommendation describing a person's qualifications and dependability.

Serbian—coming from Serbia, a historical region in central and northern Yugoslavia.

Slavs—people of eastern Europe or Asian Russia.

spectrum—the range of colors or wavelengths of radiation, including light.

theorems—statements that can be proven using logical reasoning.

Yiddish—a language spoken primarily by Jews in Eastern Europe. It is a mix of Old German combined with Hebrew and is written in the Hebrew alphabet.

Bibliography

Brennan, Richard P. *Heisenberg* Probably *Slept Here: The Lives, Times, and Ideas of the Great Physicists of the 20th Century.* New York: John Wiley & Sons, Inc., 1997.

Brian, Denis. *Einstein: A Life.* New York: John Wiley & Sons, Inc., 1996.

Calaprice, Alice. *The New Quotable Einstein.* New Jersey: Princeton University

Press and The Hebrew University of Jerusalem, 2005.
Charlesworth, Kate, and John Gribbin. *The Cartoon History of Time.* New York: Plume, 1990.

Clark, Ronald W. *Einstein: The Life and Times.* New York: Avon Books, 1971.

Einstein, Albert, Helen Dukas, and Banesh Hoffmann, *Albert Einstein: The Human Side.* New Jersey: Princeton University Press, 1979.
————. *Ideas and Opinions.* New York: Crown, 1954, 1982.
————. *Out of My Later Years.* New York: Random House, 1956.
————. *Relativity: The Special and the General Theory.* New York: Crown ,1961.

Fölsing, Albrecht. *Albert Einstein, A Biography.* New York: Penguin, 1997.

Fox, Karen C., and Aries Keck. *Einstein A to Z.* Hoboken, NJ: John Wiley & Sons, Inc., 2004.

Galison, Peter. *Einstein's Clocks, Poincaré's Maps: Empires of Time.* New York: W. W. Norton & Company, 2003.

Walker, Martin. *America Reborn: A Twentieth-Century Narrative in Twenty-six Lives*. New York: Alfred Knopf, 2000.

Wolfson, Richard. *Simply Einstein: Relativity Demystified*. New York: W. W. Norton & Company, 2003.

About the Author

A graduate of the University of Mary Washington and the University of Iowa, Tabatha Yeatts enjoys learning about the universe and everything in it from her Maryland home, which she shares with her husband, three children, and three pets. She is the author of *The Holocaust Survivors* and *Forensics: Solving the Crime*, as well as dozens of newspaper and magazine articles. Like Einstein, she's not fond of combing her hair.

Image Credits